The LAZY Princess

The quick and easy way to look fabulous and be amazing at everything

Hannah Sandling

metro

Published by Metro Publishing
an imprint of John Blake Publishing Ltd
3 Bramber Court, 2 Bramber Road,
London W14 9PB, England

www.johnblakepublishing.co.uk

First published in hardback in 2009

ISBN: 978 1 84454 761 6

British Library Cataloguing-in-Publication Data:

A catalogue record for this book is available from the British Library.

Design by www.envydesign.co.uk

Printed and bound by 🐾 Grafica Veneta S.p.A., Trebaseleghe (PD) - Italy.

1 3 5 7 9 10 8 6 4 2

Papers used by John Blake Publishing are natural, recyclable products made from
wood grown in sustainable forests. The manufacturing processes conform to the
environmental regulations of the country of origin.

Interior photographs reproduced courtesy of Rex Features, with the exception of
those on pages 146 and 162.

ABOUT THE AUTHOR

Hannah Sandling is a television presenter, writer, leading fashion stylist and interior designer. Her credits include *Clutter Nutters* (CBBC), *60 Minute Makeover* (ITV), *Teenagers' Guide To Life* (BBC Switch) and *Pop Goes the Band* (Living) and she has commentated live from the red carpet for prestigious award ceremonies including the BAFTAs and the Oscars.

Hannah has commented and styled for many magazines including *Heat*, *Mizz*, *Tatler*, *Elle*, *GQ*, *Grazia*, *Closer*, *In Style*, *Cosmo*, *Polo Cartier*, *Wedding* and *Your Home,* and she has worked with various celebrities including Duncan James, Kirsty Gallacher, Katie Price, Jenny Frost, Sienna Miller, Dita Von Teese, Emma Bunton and Jamelia. She has also worked with brands including M&S, Tampax, The Earring Boutique, Dove, Gumtree and Boots.

Hannah has a BA (Hons) degree in Art and Design and has exhibited her work at the National Gallery. She is a self-confessed workaholic and loves nothing more than running marathons, horse riding, travelling and playing tennis. She keeps her energy levels high by having early nights, drinking lots of water and eating plenty of choccie.

I mention candles on quite a few occasions because I love the gorgeous ambience that they create. Please, girlies, be safe when using them and, if you are going on a date with a boy, then be super careful and **ALWAYS** make sure someone knows where you are and who you are with. It's always cooler to be careful than not. And if cabs are your chosen mode of transport, make sure you go with a reputable company. Arrange a time and a safe place to be picked up, and make sure you know the cab driver's name and car registration.

Acknowledgements

Thankfully, this book wasn't too hard to create as my mobile is jam-packed with plenty of Lazy Princesses and Lazy Goddesses, all with equally lazy information that they wanted to share with me. Firstly, I would like to thank my amazing Mumma for being full of the best bone-idle tips ever and also my father for making me the independent chick that I am! I'd also like to thank my two 'Butt Head Society' sisters, Katrina and Ems, for being so supportive and full of the best goss ever! Rojy, me ol' bean! You too are just fabby dabby! Bruno – you're 'heaven on toast'. A big hug to my dog, Puppy, who I rescued from the streets in South America.

Thank you also to Diane Banks and to the John Blake publishing team – without you guys this book would not have happened. And last, but certainly not least, Sue Rider, the golden, super duper agent who just makes it all happen! Sue, you rock!! Thank you so much for being so incredible in every way!

Contents

INTRODUCTION   xiii

1 WARDROBE WORKOUT   1

2 HEALTHY LIVING   81

3 SPARKLE LIKE A PRINCESS   117

4 MIDNIGHT FEASTS, STYLISH SPAS &   181
     SUCCESSFUL SLEEPOVERS

5 FAB FRIENDSHIPS   205

6 FESTIVAL FEVER FOR EVERY DIVA   215

7 BE AN ECO CHICK   235

8 FROGS AND TOADS... AND YUMMY PRINCES   247

LAZY PRINCESS SHOPPING LIST   277

Introduction

FAR, FAR AWAY, deep inside a place called home is a snarly, grumpy old sloth who lives in a bottomless pit filled to the brim with crisp packets, smelly old socks, used tissues, down-at-heel shoes and thousands of girly gossip magazines. For the few brave enough to dare to walk over the threshold and enter the dark dungeon… well, they know only too well that the only form of communication is burping, grunting or farting!

The tired-looking wardrobe spends its life moaning and groaning from all the old clutter and clobber that it's fed on a daily basis; piled high with junk and jewellery, the sweet little chair hasn't been sat on since it can remember, and as for the carpet… Well, that hasn't seen daylight for the past ten years! Does this sound like a familiar story?

But now the Lazy Goddess has come to your rescue with the genie in her handbag! So wake up, you sleeping beauties out there, and step forth from your castle. As of today, you're going to achieve all of your hopes and love your life beyond your wildest dreams. Yes, all you aspiring Lazy Princesses everywhere, I'm the keeper of the golden key to success! I'm

going to show you how to create potions and lotions from the secret vaults of your house: I'll tell you about the pizza-face fixers available for those fed up with staying at home and squeezing their zits while everyone else is out snogging; I'll explain how to deal with those dreaded wardrobe fiascos and I'll share with you how to make your bedroom look like a palace fit for a real princess, ready for when your best mates come over. Plus, I'll show you how to bag yourself a seriously hot Prince Charming and how to get yourself a whole new wardrobe without having to spend a single penny!

Josephine Odushoga, Mount Carmel RC Technology College for Girls, London

1

Wardrobe Workout

I ONCE TURNED on MTV *Cribs*, you know, the show where you get to sneak around the house of someone who is mega-famous, and I remember sitting there for twenty minutes, green with envy, mouth wide open and dribbling and drooling all over the place at an exclusive guided tour of Mariah Carey's unbelievable wardrobe. She didn't just have a couple of wardrobes to put her bits and bobs into, but an entire floor was dedicated to housing the most saliva-inducing clothes. It was like you'd just stumbled into all your favourite shops in one go! Her underwear was hung up, each piece on a little silk hanger, and her zillion pairs of shoes were caressed and parked up like little Cadbury's chocolate fingers, and what's more, they even had their own maid for 24/7 TLC on tap. How insane, but totally fab!

Sadly, most of us don't live like this, with our clothes all colour coded and sorted out into seasons. The majority have wardrobes that resemble a burgled flea market, with clothes exploding out of drawers, every handle, hook, door and chair covered in a dress, top or necklace, etc. and shelves groaning and puffing under the weight of the clutter you've managed to bury away for the past decade. As for the carpet, what on earth does it look like? No wonder most of us chicks always moan that we never have anything to wear. Trying to find the right outfit would be like setting out on an archaeological expedition!

If this sounds like you, then you desperately need to work out your wardrobe – NOW!

ORGANISE YOUR WARDROBE

- Once a week, open your wardrobe doors and bedroom windows and have a cold blow-through of air to freshen up your clothes.
- Don't over-cram your wardrobe either, otherwise the clothes won't be able to breathe properly and they'll start to smell stale.
- To stop a little job becoming a mammoth one, tidy your wardrobe and bedroom floor once a day. And no, I don't mean you should just open up a cupboard and kick anything and everything inside it! When you come home from school, rather than lobbing all your clothes and accessories on to the bed or floor, actually hang them up and put all your accessories back in their relevant homes. That way, they will never pile up and you'll always find what you're looking for.
- Use dead space (space not normally used for anything) cleverly to store items. Ask an adult to bang a nail in the back of your wardrobe door and hang a bag on it, filled with little nick-nacks usually stuffed to the back of the wardrobe or stashed away on the floor under the bed somewhere.
- Actually, the space underneath your bed is another brilliant place for storing things. I have two boxes on wheels under mine. When I need something, I simply wheel it out, rather than having to commando it by crawling under the bed

myself – which usually results in me getting stuck for at least ten minutes!

- Wardrobe organisation can save precious minutes when they're most needed. Hang all your skirts, trousers and shirts, etc. in their own little departments.

- When you take off your clothes at night, empty the pockets of tissues, sweet papers and anything else that you may have stashed away in there. There are three reasons for this: it will stop your clothes from moulding into a permanent lumpy shape, allows them to breathe and you (or your mum) won't have to pick out the gooey mess left behind post-washing machine.

- The way we chuck our belts into the wardrobes without a care in the world would indicate that we think they are spaghetti. Belts should not be mistreated: they're very important, almost life-changing accessories. Not only do they make an outfit look finished off and super-cool, they also make our bums look a lot smaller if worn correctly so find a good home for them! If you're pushed for space, again, ask an adult to bang some nails in the back of your wardrobe door, then hang them up neatly, out of the way of their buckles.

- I have heaps of funky costume jewellery that I've collected over the years and, if it wasn't for my brilliant transparent mini drawers from Muji, I don't know where I'd be! Simply stack them on top of each other, filled with your goodies, and when you need to find something, you won't have to trawl through every single box or bag because you can just peer in through the sides of the drawers to see exactly what you want.

- I know what it's like when you've got a new garment: you wear it to death – literally. So rather than sending it to an early grave, don't wear your togs day after day! Not only will your friends get fed up of seeing you in the same thing, but repeated wear actually makes your clothes stretch out of shape, so keep your wardrobe circulating.

- Did you know that 30% of handbags are contaminated with faecal matter (poo)? Probably because we dump our poor little bags on the floor when we go into a public loo. There are two solutions for this: either clean your bag with a facial wipe, or hang it on the back of the door or around your neck – *anything* to avoid having to sit it on top of other people's poo particles! It's either that or the germs will be picked up on your hands, which could then transfer to your mouth or eyes, and you might end up with a stomach bug. Nice!

- No one sane enjoys ironing, so help your poor mum out by not cramming millions of garments into your wardrobe so that they won't have anywhere to move or breathe. The more you ram in, the more creases your clothes will have, meaning the more ironing you or your mum will have to do. Look at it this way: if your mum has a constant stream of clothes to iron day after day, which she has to juggle with running the family household, and perhaps a job too, she might just give you an ironing lesson if it all becomes too much. So, be thoughtful, and keep your ironing to a minimum!

- Hoover out the bottom of your wardrobe every few months to keep the dust from settling.

- Don't go adding a stinky item of clothing to your wardrobe immediately after taking it off – especially if you've just been to a barbecue and your clothes smell of smoky burgers, or you've paid a visit to the chip shop! Instead, place them on a hanger and hang it up on the doorframe or by an open window to air for the night. That way, you'll prevent all of those food smells from stinking out the rest of your wardrobe!

- Pop scrunchy hair bobbles in along with your regular wash every week – they can get very smelly and skanky-looking. I always chuck mine in one of those little mesh laundry bags that come free with your washing machine tablets – this will protect them and stop them from tangling all of your clothes up into one big ball.

- Moth holes are great if you really want to look grungy like a tramp but, if you don't, then put lavender bags in your wardrobe to keep the moths at bay.

- If there's anything you no longer like or need, ask your mum to wash and iron it first, then bag it up and hotfoot it down to your local charity shop. Err, and NO knickers, thank you, girlies! Or how about asking your parents if they can help you organise a car boot sale to shift some of your old unwanted clobber and raise some extra cash for new goodies. Put the word out so that you have loads of punters rocking up with their cash. You can also sell your old bits on eBay. Again, ask your parents to help out here – not just because they can help you navigate around the site, but also because you might need their permission to sell some of your stuff.

- Padded hangers are a must when it comes to hanging your delicate tops. You can always do a homemade job by re-cycling old shoulder pads (ask your mum if she has any still kicking around from the eighties). Just stick them to the ends of hangers.

- Another good way to make your own padded hanger is to cover a metal one with any spare bubble wrap hanging around the house. Tightly wrap it around the hanger and secure in place with some clear sticky tape.

- Try to match all of your hangers. Bizarrely, hangers that look the same psychologically encourage you to keep your wardrobe tidy.
- Pretty underwear is a great way to boost your mood and confidence, so chuck out any grubby or greying knickers and bras, or any with the elastic hanging out. Good underwear doesn't have to be expensive, so there's no excuse for those skiddy pants lurking around in your drawer.
- If you have delicate clothes (lace and silks, etc.) that you want to place in your wardrobe, always hang them inside out so they won't snag on a neighbouring sequinned top.
- Put your smart coats and jackets into long clothes bags and hang them up. This will keep the light from discolouring them and prevent dust from settling too.
- When storing clothes under your bed or above the wardrobe, always put them in airtight bags to keep them fresh and to prevent moths from getting too cosy and building homes in them.
- A multiple skirt or trouser hanger that you hang inside one end of your wardrobe is a great way of storing lots of things on one hanger and it's a brilliant way of saving precious space too.
- If your shoes are beginning to look like those that you see randomly in the gutter, then it's time to lob them, I'm afraid, no matter how special they are. Skanky shoes won't do you any favours! However, if you do want the little blighters to stay around for a bit longer then get them re-heeled/re-soled regularly. This will prevent them from wearing out too quickly.
- You should never hang a lovely jumper on the washing line with pegs because it will lose its shape. Instead, use a clean broom handle: push it through one cuff and out the other then suspend it on something that is safe and off

the floor (between two trees, or between two tall chairs, or even between two open windows where you can balance the broom on the top of each window) and leave to dry.

- Always hang your trousers from the hem. Not only will they hang straighter, but it's actually quicker than hanging them from the waistband.

- The heavier the item of clothing, the stronger the hanger should be – this applies to winter coats especially.

- You know those funny little loops that you always find inside a garment, usually just underneath the armpit? Well, they're there for a reason and should definitely be used for hanging, where possible. Fabric support straps help to take the stress away and keep tops in shape.

- A good way to update an ageing coat is to change the buttons for some cool and funky ones or maybe sew a really unusual trim on to the pockets. A little facelift on your clothes can totally transform them, almost like having new ones.

- Never reuse those plastic clothes bags that you get from the dry cleaners to store your garments. They will stop your clothes from breathing and start to smell. Instead, store them in fabric clothes bags.

- Similarly, don't try to reuse the horrid wire hangers that your mum probably collects from the dry cleaners. They offer no support whatsoever for your clothes. Also, they create an indentation and, if they rust, then your clothes will become stained.

- In summer we don't need our heavy winter clothes, and in winter light and airy garments are unsuitable. Whatever season you're in, it's a good idea to stash away the stuff you're not going to wear in airtight bags but always clean your clothes beforehand or the smells and dirt will become embedded and your clothes will fester away.

● When it's conker season, go and collect at least 30 of them. Why? Well, you need some for playing conkers, of course, and the rest can be used to keep horrid clothes-eating moths away. All you have to do is lob them anywhere in your wardrobe and in drawers. Believe me, it's the equivalent of us human beings having to eat a shed load of Brussels... Ugh!

HOW TO DETOX YOUR CLOTHES-GUZZLING WARDROBE

I'm all for a detox session when it comes to our wardrobes, for two reasons. Firstly, a clutter-free and streamlined closet equals a more stylish princess, as you will always be able to pick out something with ease, rather than having to wade through a stream of dense, forest-like clobber. Secondly, the more oldies you get rid of (items of clothing you no longer need or love), the more dosh you can raise to buy new delights. There are a few things that you can do with your old clobber. You can put it on eBay, you can be an angel and take it to your local charity shop or you can organise a clothes-swapping party with the girls one evening, so that you all get new and fun things to wear without having to spend a penny. Before you do any of these things, make sure you get your parents' permission.

I have to warn you that clearing the oldies out of your closet can be a very painful experience, even more heartbreaking than missing an episode of *Gossip Girl*. So, you need to book yourself a little shopping trip to get some new clobber to cheer you up (with all the money that you've raised from selling your old cast-offs on eBay or from your car boot sale). Or you could get a big box of chocolates, or a bucket-load of scrummy sweet strawberries and share them with a friend, who can reassure you that you did the right thing by selling your clothes.

Here's how to blitz your wardrobes, girlies! Start off by emptying everything you own on to your bed and then pick up each item, one by one, and put it into one of the two piles – and be honest!

Keep-Me Pile

- Coats and jackets – key investments, they will keep you warm as toast in winter (unless it's a summer trench coat, of course). These are clothes that you can see yourself keeping for ages but, if you purchase an unusual colour or print, it will age quickly. So buy in a plain colour like black, beige, dark blue or brown. That way, you can wear it year in, year out, plus it will go with anything. From time to time, you can always change the look of it by adding brooches, scarves and badges, or you could even swap the buttons for something outrageously funky.
- A blazer – instantly puts the smart into casual.
- Basic foundation pieces, such as white, grey, black and beige T-shirts that can easily be jazzed up with cool accessories. These can be as cheap as chips and replaced any time. White shirts for work needn't be boring – choose ones with ruffles and bows.
- Stuff you love and treasure – little nick-nacks from foreign market stalls, as well as granny's cast-offs, transform dull-looking outfits and look unusual.
- Cardigans – always useful to throw over a casual look with jeans or to work with a dress; have a mixture of plain and patterned/striped.

- One of the most trusted friends in your wardrobe is the little black dress! Vital in any girl's wardrobe, LBDs are a long-lasting trend. They can be easily and radically transformed with accessories, belts and sashes. They just don't have a sell-by date, which means you can wear it year in, year out by just switching funky accessories – and no one will know you have the same frock on! If that isn't a great money-saving tip, I don't know what is!

- Your most flattering jeans – one light, one medium colour, one dark and, of course, a pair of skinnies! Day and night, jeans are brilliant as they can be dressed up or down.

- Fun, chic glammy pammy dresses that can be thrown on for hot parties – great for when you need to impress a fittie!

- WAG-style sunglasses – throw them on for instant footy-fabulous fashion! Remember, the bigger the better.

- Denim minis – yes, please! During the summer, you can get them out to show off your sun-kissed tan and through the chilly winter months you can throw on some chunky woolly tights and wear them with really cool boots!

- Ballet pumps – pump up the vibe, baby! A stylish chick's wardrobe would not be complete without a few of these scattered around the place. Colours look great, as do patents and tartans, etc. They are the best way to put some punch into an outfit while keeping your feet flat and happy. I've got a great little black pair that have flexible, squidgy soles, meaning I can roll them up and tuck them neatly into my handbag for when my feet get tired of wearing heels. They really are a welcome treat for my little tootsies.

- Wedge sandals – these streamline your leggies, look hot and they're easy to walk in.

- Winter boots – we love 'em! Stock up on styles in black or brown, but make sure they're of good quality because you'll

be wearing these little babies half the year. Wear them with skinny jeans, tights and cute hippy dresses, etc.

- A cool clutch in a classic colour – it's a must-have! You can always change the look of it by attaching different clasps or brooches.
- A big tote bag for the daytime so you can carry the kitchen sink around with you; choose one in a funky colour or metallic finish for a bit of wow celeb factor.
- A cap or headscarf is a must for bad hair days.
- Belt up – fake a waist/hourglass figure with belts that can be worn over cardigans, dresses and jeans. Have a chain belt too – looks hot over fitted dresses.
- Accessories literally party by themselves and are the tools of a rising style star. They maketh an outfit plus prevent you getting lost in a crowd. Make sure you stock up on rings, necklaces, scarves, earrings and bracelets, etc.
- Undies – keep all good-quality, skid-free knickers and tatter-free bras. Remember, underwear is just as important as outerwear – it's what holds up the rest of your outfit, after all! Every underwear drawer should have a black bra and knickers (so you can wear them with a black outfit), a white bra and knickers, nude bra and knickers, strapless bra and seamless knickers – that way you'll have the most failsafe underwear ever for all outfits and occasions.

What to Throw Away
- Clothes that make you look like a tent.
- Garments which pinch in all the wrong places.
- Anything that's on its last legs and hanging on by a thread.
- Clothes you've never worn, or at least not for the last three years.

- Garments that drain the colour from your complexion and make you look tired.
- Scuffed shoes.
- Anything stained, or with faded colour, or that has been mangled in the wash.

CATWALK CREATIONS

Customising, turning something old into something new, is the cheapest way of getting a fashion fix. Not only does it get your creative juices flowing but it also allows you to create unique one-off pieces that no one else has. From your granny's to your parents', raid every attic you can get yourself into in the search for juicy little finds that you can throw into the fashion mix for a seamless look.

- There's nothing worse than someone else rocking up to the party and you're both wearing the same dress, so make yours stand out in the crowd. Add some excitement, such as ribbon around the edge of the hemline base, or attach a big flower (corsage) on to the side of it. If it's a strapless dress, consider adding some homemade shoulder straps created from a string of beads.
- Make your arm candy (handbag) devilishly charming by adding character! Clip irresistible jewels, little tassels, mini purses, cute charms, buddha heads or whatever else takes your fancy onto the straps. This makes it original and gives it a personality of its own.
- Brooches aren't just for grumpy old grannies! They are also for drab-looking coats that could do with a bit of cheering up. Attach them to one of the lapels or, if you want to be really inventive, pop a headscarf on your hair (as you do when you put freshly washed hair up in a wet towel) and

clip the brooch onto the front of it, just above your forehead. Now that's very chic, sweetie darling!

- You might also flick some fabric paint at your bag or pick up a fun stencil from your local art store and create a really cool design with it. This is a great idea, especially if you love your bag to bits, but it has a stain on it. Any little imperfections will be covered up a treat.

- Fabric pens are lots of fun too – just pop the lid off and scribble an arty, Picasso-like design over your plain T-shirt or jeans. If you already have a design in mind, draw it out on a piece of paper beforehand so you know exactly what you want to do. To make your T design really show up, do it on a white or light-coloured T. Now, the important thing to bear in mind is don't draw straight on to the actual T without wedging a bit of cardboard in between the front and back (I use an old cereal box). If you don't do this, the pen will leak through to the other side. Once you've drawn your design on to the T, iron it. This will set it. The pen packaging will include details of settings for iron temperatures.

- I love to collect beautiful fabrics from market stalls everywhere and then introduce them into my wardrobe. You can customise an old top or a skirt by sewing a piece of gorgeous material on to it, therefore making a one-off piece! Ooh and don't forget to check with your mum to see if it's OK to shred an item of clothing apart first, just in case it's a family heirloom that's got loads of historic value! Whoops!

- So, what are the three ingredients that make an outfit come to life? Good posture (bum in, chest out, head held high), good attitude (being happy and positive) and a huge sprinkling of confidence. (Even if you don't feel confident, fake it! Eventually it will become real.)

Original art

How about a bit of tie-dyeing? It looks awesome, so arty and original, plus it's a great way of giving an old friend a bit of a boost (a T-shirt, in this case) in the style department. Here's how to do it.

First, this is a job that needs to be done miles away from your parents' lovely carpet. They may want to throttle you if dye gets anywhere near it! So, for that reason, I suggest you head outside with a bucket, your chosen colour of coldwater dye, T-shirt (100% cotton works best) and rubber gloves (blue or red hands might be a little too scary!). Cover yourself up so you don't splatter your good clothes (I always pierce a bin liner and put it over my head and wear it like a poncho).

Fill your bucket up with the recommended amount of warm water (check the dye packet for instructions). Dissolve and mix in your powdered dye, along with 6 tablespoons salt (or whatever the instructions recommend). Leave to cool down. Get your T-shirt and some string (or elastic bands). Make a small bunch of the fabric and tie the string around the bottom. Now cut the string. Repeat on other places across the T, then get the string and wrap it four times around the whole T to make a parcel bundle. Plunge the T in the dye concoction and leave for 30 minutes. Stir occasionally with a twig or an old chopstick so you know the whole thing is submerged under the mixture.

Take the T out, squeeze out the excess liquid from the fabric and rinse under cold running water until it runs clear. Peg it up on your washing line (or lay flat on some newspaper) and leave to dry thoroughly. When bone dry, untie the string to see your brilliant work but, before you wear it, wash it separately in the washing machine on a cool setting (ask your mum first), and leave to dry away from direct sunlight. After all that, you'll have one seriously cool piece of kit to parade about in!

- Hair bands and hair clips are the fashionable must-have for any outfit and make you shine out in a crowd. To make yours look super-original or less plain, customise it! Using art glue, apply new ribbons, bows, gems and buttons, etc. Basically, anything that looks cute!
- To glamorise your mobile phone or iPod with a bit of tinseltown glitz, cover it in glass beads or rhinestones.
- Don't lob out that old pair of jeans! Cut the legs off and turn them into a hip pair of Kate-Moss-at-Glastonbury-style jean shorts (easy peasy that – just chop off the leg material to the length you want the shorts – simple when you know how!), or make them into a mini and add some embellishments such as ribbons, badges, buttons, patches, etc.
- Cover a boring satchel with lots of really cool and catchy-looking badges.
- Tassled or diamante key rings are a style addict's top secret. Buy one bag and change the look of it every time with different attachments.

- Keep your nose stuck in weekly fashion magazines and websites. Try to absorb what's in fashion and ideas that come straight off the catwalk. Let this inspire you to create your own pieces and work them into your existing closet.

- You could use a little scarf not just for your hair, but also as an alternative idea to a bracelet. Simply wind it round your wrist and tie the ends together.

- To keep up at the top of the fashion radar, how about jazzing up your boring wellies? Get a fun-looking stencil from an art store and then, using acrylic paint, dab on the design just on the sides or all over each boot.

- Take your artistic licence and give your old jeans or T-shirt a winning abstract streak. Go outside, cover the ground in newspaper and splatter fabric paint at your clobber using a twig or a paintbrush. This will give clothes that you're bored with a seriously cool vibe. Only seriously minded rockers need apply, though! It's a particularly good idea if you can't get a stain out of your favourite pair of jeans. Just add a bit more art and no one will ever know!

- Never throw out old buttons. In fact, collect them and after a while you'll be able to string yourself a really unusual, trendsetting bracelet. Or you can take off horrible buttons from an item of clothing and sew on your gorge new ones instead.

- Second-hand stores and charity shops are the best places to pick up cheap (and often very stylish) new bits, but don't worry if they don't always fit. Take the items home and alter or customise them to your liking. Customising might be easy whereas altering isn't. So either ask your mum very nicely if she might be able to do the job or show you how to, or ask her to take you down to your local dry cleaners where they usually have people who can do the job for you at a very low cost.

- If your beady eyes spot a beautiful dress when you're out shopping at a market, charity shop or second-hand store and you don't like the style, but you LOVE the trim, the buttons or the lace detailing, get it! Take it home, cut off the pieces that you do like and then sew them on to something you already own, like a pair of jeans or a dress.

- Car boot sales are worth their weight in gold, they really are! They're rammed full of dirt-cheap clothes and clobber. Personally, I like to buy clothes that don't necessarily fit or look nice as they stand, but have seriously cool details that I can cut off and sew on to something I already have at home, ready for a bit of customising. Look out for buttons, cute trims, belts, lace, etc. You never know, that bit of lace on a shirt might just look amazing sewn on to the back pockets of a pair of jeans, or the cute trim could be stunning around the top of the neckline of a plain jacket.

- Buy a variety of pretty fabric butterflies and pin, clip or sew them on to your dress, hat or handbag.

SWAPPING SESSIONS

Organise a swapping session with your fellow chicks. If you fancy having your wardrobe stocked up to the brim with lots of lovely new things without having to part with a single penny of your hard-earned pocket money, it's just the solution. It's a free shopping spree (swapping session) with your fashionista best friends, direct from the living-room carpet! This creative way of re-styling and updating your wardrobe is also the perfect excuse to get the girls over for a good old gossip and giggle. Here's how to throw the coolest swapping session in town and get some new stitches.

Sex and the City-style non-alcoholic cocktails

I love these mocktails! They're totally delish and a must for any swapping session to keep those energy levels high.

Chicky Chocana

Serves 1

450ml milk

30g dark chocolate, broken into pieces

2 ripe bananas, peeled and roughly chopped

Heat up the milk in a small saucepan, never allowing it to boil. Now stir in the chocolate until dissolved. Pop the choccie milk and bananas into a blender and blast until yummy and smooth. Pour into a tall glass and serve at once. Don't forget to doll it up with pretty cocktail decorations such as pink feathers and a strawberry wedged on the side of the glass!

Apple-licious Blueberry Delight

Serves 1

4 apples, cored and chopped

30 white seedless grapes

30 blueberries

Place them all in a blender or juicer and blast together. Pop into a chilled glass (store the glass in the fridge for a few hours beforehand to keep it cold), and jazz it up with straws, brightly coloured cocktail umbrellas and anything else that funks them up! Serve at once.

- First, set the rules. Write fun invitations to the gals you want to invite and those on the guest list are the only ones allowed in, it's a strict door policy. Make sure everyone replies, so that you know how many people will be coming.

- Where will you host your party? The living room, your bedroom, even the garden on a hot sunny day are all good options. Before you organise it, check with your parents first. It sounds obvious, but make sure everybody brings clothes to the party that they no longer need or wear and that they are in good condition with no tears or buttons missing.

- Work out in advance whether the swapping of an item of clothing is temporary or permanent. You don't want to take something thinking it's yours to customise, only to then be told they want it back.

- If you're only swapping temporarily, make sure you take full responsibility for anything borrowed. If you damage anything, you must replace it. Also, make sure that you return everything washed or dry cleaned, ironed and generally in good condition, plus you return it all on an agreed date.

- Decide how many items everyone should bring and how much they're worth. That way, no one gets a bad deal. Your friends will either need to be the same size as you, or you will need to invite a mix of friends so that everyone has at least someone of the same size or shape as themselves.

- Only exchange things that you really don't wear any more. No sad regrets, OK?

- On the day, transform your room or garden into a girly haven with candles (remember never to leave candles unattended), incense, sweets, snacks, pretty flowers and make-up. Create a catwalk using sheets or a long entrance hall rug, so you can all strut your stuff. Set up some chairs or a pile of squidgy cushions or pillows either side of the catwalk so the trendy audience has somewhere to sit.

- Don't forget your camera to capture the fashion-savvy moments.
- Stock up on healthy snacks (mixed fruit kebabs are perfect for the fashion crowd) – remember, modelling can be hungry work!
- Don't forget to wear your huge WAG-style sunglasses on the day – so what if you can't see a thing, it's the look that's more important! Styling and curating a show is an important role and therefore you need to be looking super-stylish and glamorous.

GET THE VIBE GOING!

Upbeat music is a must for any party. Line up the CDs so you have something to strut your stuff to as you take it in turns to shimmy down the catwalk like a superstar. Have a digital camera on standby: ask one of your friends to take pictures from all angles to see how you look in your newfound treasure; it's perfect for documenting the event too, then you can hold another video party to watch it all over again! Ask your buddies to bring their iPods along so that you have a good, eclectic mix of music.

LOOK SIZZLING HOT IN ALL YOUR PHOTOS

How many times have you collected your prized photos from the shop only to find you've got zombie-like red eyes or you look like you're about to cry and then there's the double chin – where did that spring from? Anyhow, when you're sitting or standing around, waiting with a fixed 'cheesed' grin' while one of your parents fumbles about with the camera trying to work out where the 'on' button is, you can start to feel a bit of a dork, right? Here's how to look picture perfect every time your mug comes face to face with the camera lens. Before you know it, you'll be a pro like Paris Hilton and Kate Moss!

- Step 1: Speedily apply some lippy gloss and tousle your hair into place. Do the teeth check by doing a gorilla grin at someone and ask them if you have anything stuck in there. Having a grin littered with spinach really isn't that good a look!
- Step 2: Relax all of your muscles. Have the photographer count 1, 2, 3, then breathe in on one and exhale on three. This will make you look comfortable and chilled out.
- Step 3: Have you noticed how Victoria Beckham almost always looks miserable in her photos? Well, it's because she overpouts in every pose, making her look cheesed off 24/7. Instead, give off a gentle smile with a tiny bit of pouting to look happy and natural.
- Step 4: Eyes are indeed the windows to our souls and say a lot about how we are feeling, so the general rule here is no squinting. Although you might think it looks smoky and seductive, you'll just look like you're about to fall asleep. No over-opening them like big saucers, either. You'll only end up looking as if you've guzzled way too many choccie biscuits and penny sweets and are having a sugar high! Keep your eyes happy and relaxed. Photographers that I have worked with always advise to 'smile through your eyes'.
- Step 5: Shoulders back, bum in, boobies out and stand lovely and tall (you should feel as if someone is almost stretching you out). Rather than standing straight on to the camera, which can sometimes make you look bigger than you are, turn a little to the side. Check out glossy magazines to see

how Paris Hilton does this perfectly, with one leg crossed over in front of the other. It always flatters her and, within the celeb world, it's a trade secret.

- Step 6: To avoid looking possessed by the Devil with red eyes, don't stare straight down the camera lens. Instead, look about half a centimetre above the lens.

Now you know the basic rules, here's how to pose depending on your body shape.

Short Stumpy Legs (this is my section!)
Don't plonk yourself down on a chair right at the back. This will make your bum squidge out and your pins will look 2cm long! Instead, sit on the edge of the seat, keep your knees

---

Brendan Cole – Dancer

My girlfriend is a model and taught me this tip for posing for pictures. All you have to do is push your chin forward (not upwards) by about an inch. This will slim down your jaw-line and ensure you will never be captured with a double chin (however many you have). You should only do this for pictures taken front on. If done from the side you could be up for some serious embarrassment when the photos are produced. Practise in the mirror at home first or mess around with your camera to see what an amazing difference it makes. It's a very small thing but will ensure you always end up with beautiful holiday snaps.

together and pose with your ankles about 60–80cm apart from each other – they will magically lengthen.

Boyish Figure

You need to create shapes and you can do this through the angle of your arms or legs. So, rather than standing there like a penguin with your arms glued down by your sides, put your hands on your hips, stick your elbows out and stand with one leg slightly bent in.

Squidgy Arms

Notice how celebs never pose with their arms pressed to their sides. Instead they always hold them about 10cm away from their bods when they're having their pictures taken. This is a brilliant way to make bigger arms look smaller without anybody noticing what you're doing, plus they will then look better in the photo so you might just make the album, after all.

Blobby Tummy

If you're wearing a lush little dress or a bikini, sitting down with your body scrunched up will only accentuate the rolls, so make sure you stand up and suck your tummy in, or lie back if you're on a sun lounger on the beach. This will even out your doughy tummy. But you know what? As long as you feel happy and confident and have chosen your clothes well for your body shape and you're having a super-duper time, then you'll always look great whatever your size.

THE ICING ON THE CAKE

Clothes without accessories are a bit like going to Cornwall and having fish without the chips, summer without sunshine or Ant presenting without Dec! Accessories can also be seen like spices in the curry world: they are the key essentials for creating those delicious exotic dishes. Without them, they're just plain boring and bland to the tastebuds.

Like spices, accessories are thrown into the mix to help clothes come alive. They're also little secret weapons. Learn how to use them correctly and they'll disguise a multitude of sins. For example, you can hide your greasy barnet under a hat, or an upper-arm bangle might be just the thing to divert attention away from chipped or chewed nails. At the same time, accessories can also highlight areas you hate. A cute little ankle chain accentuates fankles (fat ankles), while a gorgeous, eyecatching necklace draws attention to your spotty chest.

Whether you want your accessories to whisper or shout, you can dramatically transform an outfit from ordinary to extraordinary or from work to party with just a few simple tweaks and a few cleverly placed items. Here's how to do it.

- Your jewellery should always be in tune with what you're wearing. A diamond necklace won't look right with a hippy outfit, nor would a little black dress work with daytime wooden bangles.
- I love, love, *love* market stalls and vintage stalls in all countries around the world! Accessories tend to be mega-cheap and won't weigh your luggage down too much. Actually, that's total rubbish when it comes to me going abroad! Every time I go to somewhere lovely like Thailand, where everything is ridiculously cheap, I always end up having to buy another suitcase to house mounds of market-stall must-haves, which all have amazing memories attached to them.
- Build snuggly little homes for all your accessories! You can be totally eco-friendly and turn egg boxes into earring holders

(one pair in each section) or transform old jam jars into bobble holders. Cover the insides and bottoms of old biscuit tins and cutlery trays with velvet (glue down with PVA). The soft material will help to protect your more precious jewels.

- If you want to glam up the outside of drab-looking boxes or tins, cover them in sparkly fabric, funky wrapping paper, glitter, meaningful photos, stick-on gems or a lick of colourful paint.
- If you have masses of accessories and want to store them all neatly, choose tins or boxes with lids so you can stack them all on top of each other in a cupboard.
- Wearing lots of gold jewellery all at once can be cheap and tacky-looking. You can only get away with it if you are going to a fancy dress party! Don't worry if you've lost one of a pair of gorge and very unusual earrings. You can always tell people it's a one-off piece of ear candy and meant to be worn like that. Don't do this with studs, though!
- If you've fallen in love with a colour but it doesn't go with your skin tone, then, rather than ditching the idea of wearing it altogether, just add hints of it around your outfit through accessories.
- Sunglasses are the LBD of the accessory world. They are as important as your lipgloss, so never leave the house without them! Wearing them makes you look like an A-lister and you can always fall back on them to hide a multitude of sins, like a very late night! When you are choosing shades, consider how big or small your face is. I always think Nicole Richie looks a little odd in some of her glasses because they're way too big for her. Big, oversized glasses add that Hollywood celeb feel to a look, but just bear in mind that they have to be in proportion to you.
- If you have a double chin, avoid wearing a choker – unless you want three extra chins on top of that!

- When your face is looking a bit under the weather and lifeless, stick on a pair of sparkly diamante earrings to brighten yourself up.

- A heavily textured handbag, such as fake snakeskin, feathers, sequins, etc. can add so much visual richness to a plain outfit.

- Have you noticed how a belt can quite often rise up your back? Well, that's because it's a straight-style belt. Opt instead for a curved belt that follows the contours of your hips and this should help it stay in place.

- The quickest way to update any outfit without having to spend a fortune is through funky accessories. Magazines are great places to get inspiration for what's in and what isn't, as well as how to successfully create a cutting-edge outfit. You can steal the style from all your fave celebs – just make sure you are following stylish ones! If you have an oblong face, you can wear big, eye-catching earrings. Avoid tiny little studs – they will make your face look even longer.

- Sometimes a cute little scarf can be just what you need to jazz up an outfit, but they also come in very handy for when you need to hide greasy hair. Plus, a gorge scarf around your neck is a great alternative way to accessorise if you don't want to wear a necklace.

- A belt can totally transform a boring outfit but, because you'll be creating a focal point around your tummy, just make sure it's in trim shape. A darker-colour belt will always be more flattering than a lighter one, too.

- If you have short legs and would like them to look longer, wear the same colour belt as your trousers/skirt.

- Never spend lots on a pair of gloves. They are like socks and you always lose one!

- Did you know that your purse or wallet has more germs than a toilet seat? Once a week, clean it with antibacterial wipes!

- If you have a round face, wear angular glasses and, if you have a long and square-looking face, opt for round glasses.
- It's amazing how changing your accessories (flat shoes and plastic jewellery to high heels and sparkling goodies) totally transforms a dress from day to night.
- Matching your bag with your shoes is sooooooo naff!
- Only wear a gorgeous, attention-grabbing ring if your hands are worth showing off!
- Umbrellas can be just the item any girl needs to make her outfit look splendidly stylish, but what a task it is to open them up on a windy day! They turn inside out, they can clock you on the head and then, after fighting with your brolly all day, you leave it on the bus! Always open a brolly in the opposite direction to the wind so it's blowing towards you; the other way and you'll be doing a Mary Poppins impression across the street! Walk with your brolly facing into the wind. If you hit a sudden change in the direction of the wind (often on a street corner), pull the brolly to the ground and regain control.
- If you have Goliath-sized bones, you're better off wearing slightly chunkier jewellery than someone with Twiglets for bones, who suits more delicate jewellery.
- Sweet little bows are so quirky and cute! Pop some in your hair.

SHOE CANDY

I remember so clearly what it was like when I was a kid, staring at the classroom clock, itching for the hands to tick-tock faster so that I could leave my desk and cruise up, Ferrari-style, to the local sweet shop to spend all my pocket money!

From the outside, the sweet shop looked like a rundown old cowshed and you wouldn't even give it a second glance, but those who simply passed by had no idea what they were missing out on. Inside, it was nothing but sheer bliss and excitement with explosions of colour and whizzy, fizzy, eyepopping treats in larger-than-life glass jars. Candy heaven!

Now that I'm older I've come to realise that the feeling of giddy excitement that you get when you're buying sweets is exactly the same as when you treat yourself to a pair of new shoes. Whether buying shoes or sweets, your piggy bank is still left looking a bit sorry for itself! That's why I've come to the conclusion that shoes really are candy for us girls and, when we get a sweet or shoe craving, there's only one way to satisfy it and that's to give in! But of course, it's far healthier on our piggy banks and on our bodies not to be greedy by having the lot. Be selective, choose well and enjoy your occasional treat time.

SHOES VERSUS SWEETS

Here's a rundown of all the styles available when you want to give your feet a sweet little treat.

- Clogs: Like fudge squares, they're rich, creamy, sturdy and a guaranteed scrummy mouthful that you won't want to share with anyone! Like Marmite, you either love 'em or hate 'em. Personally I'm not a huge fan, but those who are always say they wear them when they're feeling really happy, quietly confident and want to feel comfy enough when getting on with a pile of errands.
- Ballet flats: Like white mice, they're unobtrusive, dinky and delectable. Wearing ballet flats means you're a really down-to-earth girl. I love, love, love ballet flats – they really are one of the most versatile styles you can buy and they go with everything: short or long skirts, shorts, trousers, jeans, etc., etc.
- Sparkly stilettos are fizzy cola bottles. They always create

waves of dizzy excitement to the head – great for when you want to jazz up boring outfits.

- Long boots: An all-rounder, really, like chocolate-covered Brazil nuts.
- Ankle boots are pink piggies. Cute and cheeky, they add an edge and certain quirkiness to any outfit. Think Lady GaGa in a fifties-style frock accessorised with ankle boots.
- Biker boot: Like gobstoppers, they're not for the fainthearted! Huge round hard sweets so big you can only just get them in your mouth hence the name – and they last forever! If you're the leader of the group, biker boots will do just that.
- Court shoe: The coffee cream in the Quality Street tin! A bit boring and always the last to be eaten, nevertheless you can always rely on them to be there and they never let you down. If you want to stay in the background and let somebody else take the limelight, wear a pair of these.
- Peep-toe: Love heart! Great when you're heading out on a first date. They're sweet, flirty and romantic.
- Wedges: Like fruit gums, they're easy to handle and super-yummy!
- Platforms: Flying saucers for when you need that little lift in life, they're simple on the outside, yet unbelievably tasty and tangy in the middle! The only problem is knowing when to stop.
- Cowboy boots: Banana candy, yee har, they're bundles of fun! Like the sweet, anyone wearing these is a truly fun and fruity person to be around.
- Kitten heels: Like sherbet pips, kitten heels come in a range of mouthwatering colours. They're perfect for when you're halfway between wanting to melt into the background or being the centre of attention.

- Flip-flops: Like fried eggs, they're cheap and chewy with a cool sensation! Can be enjoyed any time, day or night, and always a hit when you're on a boring long journey or simply chilling in the summer sun!
- Thongs: A little like liquorice laces they're an unusual, but delightful hit. Definitely worth a try if you're looking for something new.
- Trainers: Liquorice torpedoes. Squidgy liquorice centre covered with a hard candy shell.
- Slippers: Foam mushrooms. You'd be a liar if you said that you didn't LOVE these! They smell as good as they taste and their super-squidgyness makes them the perfect companion for when you're at home, glued to the sofa watching a great DVD. Watch out, though, they're dangerously addictive!

KEEPING SHOES IN VIP CONDITION

OK, so we've established shoes are very expensive candy for us girlies. Cradling a new pair of twinkly shoes in our sticky mitts is guaranteed to put a Cheshire-cat-like smile on our faces. So what drives us to hunt for the biggest, sweetest and juiciest shoes?

I think we love shoes so much because, unlike clothes, which sit there lifeless until you put them on, shoes look amazing in their own right well before you've put them anywhere near your tootsies. They have a life of their own. Having a great collection of shoes is like being the owner of some stunning art installations or constantly having two walking jewellery boxes stuck to your feet making them twinkle. Plus, it doesn't matter what size or shape you are – everyone can be the owner of a lovely pair of shoes and always look good in them.

But it doesn't matter how many pairs of shoes you have, there's one rule that applies to every one of you style-savvy chicks out there and that is: if you look after your shoes, they'll look after you, so here's how to keep them in VIP condition...

- Patent shoes should be laid on a bed of velvet fabric, so line the shoebox with fabric to stop them becoming scratched.
- If you don't have room to store all of your treasured trotter covers in a wardrobe or cupboard, wrap them in old pillowcases. Once you've lobbed them to the back of the wardrobe, this will protect them and prevent further damage. You can, of course, always ask your mum if she has any shoe-cover bags going spare but don't be surprised if she says no. She probably wants to keep them for her own shoe collection!
- If your shoes have become really wet from doing sports outside or just from walking in the rain, avoid plonking them on the radiator to speed-dry as they will just end up going as hard as concrete and may end up shrinking and cracking. Instead, stuff them with newspaper and leave them overnight in a dry place, preferably near a radiator. The paper will absorb all of the moisture, leaving them dry for you to wear the next day.
- If you have the space, keep your shoeboxes and stick a Polaroid of your shoes on the outside of each one to identify them. As an easier alternative, store them in clear shoeboxes.
- To keep your shoes smelling like little flowers, pierce the box that they came in with a fork to keep the air circulating around them.
- If you are adorning your monster munch tootsies with some peep-toe shoes or any open-toe sandal for that matter, those with grub-filled, rotten-looking toes need not apply. Keep your feet in top condition and paint your nails regularly if you plan to wear peep-toe or any other open-toe shoe or sandal.

- With so many wacky wellies on offer these days, customise them so they're like little futons for your feet. And no, I haven't lost the plot! If there are any pieces of unused carpet hanging around your home, ask your parents if you can use them to make a couple of insoles to put in your boots. Believe me, they'll be so comfy that you'll be praying for rain!

- If your shoes are becoming a bit stinky, stuff them with orange peel and leave overnight.

- I don't care how sporty you are: high-heeled wedged trainers are a no-no, OK?

- Having a label or price tag stuck to the base of your shoe just isn't a good look! Simply switch your hairdryer to the hottest setting, roughly blast it really close to the label for 20 seconds then peel it off with ease.

- Vaseline works a treat on dull-looking patent shoes. Pop a little bit on a flannel or facecloth and gently rub over your shoes. Give them a little buff afterwards with the clean side of the cloth that you've just used.

- Give your shoes plenty of TLC! Don't wait until they've completely worn down to get them re-soled. Once the shoe starts to become scuffed, there's no turning back, whereas a scuffed sole can be replaced, so re-heel and re-sole your favourite shoes regularly. It'll give them a new lease of life and they'll last twice as long.

- Shoes are like humans – they need feeding! Feed them with a good polish, if you want them to look good. All leather shoes are greedy and, when a bit of polish comes their way, they'll gobble up as much as possible so only do this when you've just taken them off your tootsies. Why? Well, warm leather is more supple – great news for your leather shoes because they can suck up even more polish!

- Never, ever, put your stinky sports trainers in with your most treasured heels! Ban them from this sacred area and instead store them somewhere like the garage, or under the stairs with your wellies.

- To make your stinky trainers smell a little more fragrant, pop some fabric softener sheets into the bottom of the shoe and leave overnight.

- To keep long boots in shape and in tip-top condition, stuff them with those weird-looking plastic tree horns, a big, long bundle of tissue paper or even a few T-shirts that have seen better days! Simply roll them up, sausage-roll style, and slide into each boot.

- Ah, summer, don't you just love it? All that skipping about the fields with your hair dotted with daisies! But grass stains and pavement grime can wreak havoc with canvas shoes. Well, I've found a great way of cleaning canvas: carpet shampoo! Who would think it, eh?

- Storing long boots can take up lots of space in your wardrobe, so think clever. Keep them in the boxes that they came in and wedge them under your bed.

- Never wear the same pair of shoes day in, day out – you will wear them out. Instead, let them breathe and alternate on a daily basis.

- Baking soda isn't just a great ingredient when it comes to making cakes rise, it's also fantastic for getting rid of the stale smells that creep into your shoes. All you have to do is put some of the magic mixture on to a cotton cloth, tie it at the top and pop into your shoe. Leave for ten hours or overnight and let the magic remove the stink.

- When the ice comes out to play on the wintry pavements, so does the salt to prevent us from falling flat on our faces, which is great on one hand, as I'm not sure how cool kissing the pavement looks. On the other hand, the salt can totally ruin our leather shoes. But it's dead easy to remove these white dotty marks. Simply mix a cup of water and 1 tbsp of clear vinegar together, dip in a cloth and wipe over the marks.

- Suede shoes look so swish when they are given lots of loving care, but when they're not they can look really scruffy and can totally ruin a cool-looking outfit. So give them a little buff with a suede brush after you have worn them each time. Low-tack masking tape will also remove dirt from suede shoes. For a bit more of an intense clean, you can hold them over the steam of a freshly boiled kettle for a minute and then gently buff them with your suede brush. This will remove all of the dirt. Pop on a pair of rubber gloves, mind, so that you don't burn yourself.

TROUBLESHOOTER FOR SHOES AND BOOTS

- Uncomfortable new shoes can ruin a party and even cut your night short, so, before you give them a first outing, wear them around the house to break them in. Pop on some thick socks, slip your feet in them and walk around for as long as you can bear it. Eventually, the socks will stretch your shoes so that, when you put them on without the socks, they'll be the perfect size and pain-free.

- If your shoes are super-shiny on the soles and you're skidding around as if you're on an ice rink, rather than risk a broken leg each time you put them on, ask your mum or dad to put on a pair of rubber gloves and score the soles in diagonal directions with a pair of sharp scissors. To give the shoes some much-needed grip, ask them to rub the surface of the shoes with sandpaper until it looks rough.

Alternatively, take them to your nearest shoe-mender and ask him to glue a piece of thin rubber on the bottom of each one.

- Never suffer for the sake of fashion by buying shoes that are way too small – they will only ruin your day or evening, plus they'll give you big, bulging bunions!

- If you have a loop or a big gap in the zip of your boots, try attaching a little tassel to it. This can make your boots look really cool.

- Heavily detailed summer sandals will command a lot of attention, so make sure your feet are in tip-top condition and don't ruin the look of them.

- Do you sometimes look down at your feet and feel like two boats are transporting you about? To make big feet look smaller, avoid wearing pointy-toed shoes (they elongate your feet) and instead opt for round-toed styles instead. Light-coloured shoes will always make your feet look bigger, so opt for dark, too.

- If you have got short stumpy legs, wear platform flip-flops to add length.

- You're better off buying a new pair of shoes at the end of the day when your feet are all tired, hot and puffed up so you get a real sense of how they will fit and feel. If you do this at the beginning of the day, they may swell up later and begin to hurt. It'll be too late then to take them back to the shop to get a refund.

- Silks, satins and velvets are delicate, candy-like materials and these shoes should not be worn on a daily basis or they'll look tatty in no time at all. Save them for special occasions. If you're looking for investment shoes (basically shoes you can wear day in, day out), choose leather and suede.

- If you are out shopping for shoes that you will be wearing with tights, take a pair with you so that you can get a good idea of whether or not they fit. The same goes for socks, too.

- When you're between sizes, it's always more tricky to know which size to go for. My advice is to always pick the slightly bigger size because you can slip in a couple of gel pads to fill up the empty space around your foot. For closed-toe shoes or boots, you can go for any colour insoles, but try to match the colour of a gel pad to your sandal if you're going for an open style. Alternatively, go for transparent ones. If, however, you end up buying the smaller size of shoes, there's a slight risk that they will pinch and will spend the rest of their days in the back of your wardrobe.

- If you've got spotty legs, buy some long boots to hide the problem.

- If you find it a challenge to walk in heels but really want that extra height, try a wedge style. They'll give you loads of support, plus height, but steer away from the wedges that are super-high at the back and low at the front – they'll be just as hard to walk in as high heels! Look for variations with a thick wedge from front to back.

- Open shoes and slingbacks add length to your legs and are especially useful if you have fankles (fat ankles).

- If the balls of your feet have become sore from wearing high heels, pop some gel pads in your shoes. They really will take some of the pain away.

- Kitten heels are the most versatile shoe and will take your tootsies from day to evening.

- If you are a little shorty like me, go for shoes with an open toe at the end. Magically, they make you look a little bit taller.

- Have your feet measured at least once a year – our feet constantly change size during our lifetime.

- I love a little rummage around a vintage store or even a

charity shop for second-hand clothes, bags and jewellery etc, but I definitely draw the line at previously worn shoes. Why? Firstly because they've been sweated in – nice! And secondly, they will have already moulded into the shape of the previous owner, and will therefore not fit my feet correctly.

BAGS OF FUN OR BAG LADY?

It's your choice: you can cruise around looking outrageously cool, like you've just raided *Britannia High*'s prop box or you can look like you live on the pavement, surrounded by fading, broken-handled plastic bags filled to the brim with your worldly possessions. Now I know where that phrase 'kitchen sink' comes from. Once upon a time, I used to be that bag lady! I had such a collection of plastic bags (how un-eco friendly) and used to carry at least eight at a time around with me! In fact, I even kept the nicer-looking ones for best and would colour co-ordinate them with what I was wearing. Yikes! Thankfully, times have changed!

HANDBAG HINTS

- When you're looking for a new dress, you try lots on to see which looks best, right? Well, the same applies when you're on the hunt for a new handbag. It's really important that you try them on in front of a mirror to see whether they suit you or not. For example, if you're petite like Kylie Minogue, an oversized bag will just make you look as if you're carrying a suitcase around with you, so you're better off going for a smaller style.
- I always hang my little delicate evening bags on small nails on the inside of my wardrobe doors. It keeps them neat and tidy – and reduces the risks of them being trodden on or lobbed to the floor of the wardrobe, along with my shoes!

- A tidy bag means an organised mind! Your everyday bag or school satchel should have pockets on the outside and inside for your purse, iPod and mobile. If not, you'll be forever digging around and will ruin your sparkling nails.

- If your bag looks like the dog has attacked it or you've spilled dinner down it, bin it! A scruffy bag can ruin a beautifully put-together outfit.

- Don't hang leather bags by the handle to store them – they will quickly lose their shape. Instead, stuff them with old towels and rest them on a shelf.

- When buying a summer bag, make sure you check what it feels like against your skin. A scratchy fabric or basketweave may irritate your skin when you're wearing a lovely, strappy summer dress.

- Are handbags high maintenance? Yes, big time! I always store them covered in a soft bag cover or an old pillowcase. This protects them from scuffs and stops them gathering dust.

- If you're wearing a gorgeous silk or satin dress, don't carry a beaded bag! It will snag it.

- Once a month, vacuum your bag inside to keep it fresh.

- When you're out and about at lunch, don't dump your bag on the floor! Instead, put it behind your bum so it doesn't have the chance to pick up any yucky germs. Don't leave it on the loo floor either unless you want a nice layer of poo particles stuck to the bottom!

- Clean leather and patent bags regularly with anti-bacterial wipes to get rid of any germs.

- Day in, day out, I see girls ramming their gorgeous evening bags full to the brim as if they're taking them on a week's holiday! Evening bags should always be smaller than day bags, but, if you're like me and one of those chicks who likes to pack your party bag with lots of bits and bobs, you're better off opting for a bag that's slightly bigger in size. There's nothing worse than seeing a delicate bag that's bulging at the seams. And not only that, eventually the shape of the bag will be ruined, if it's overstretched.

- If you're a jammy so-and-so and you've managed to bag yourself a great summer job in an office, then it's smart bags only if the dress code is suits. Pretty summer bags or baskets will look frivolous and out of place.

- Some fancy bags with all the trimmings look great, but if you can't get into them because of all the padlocks, buckles and chains, etc., forget it! You'll be constantly struggling whenever you want to get anything out of it. Look for an everyday, runabout bag with easy access so you can dump everything in it, not one that's more like cracking a code to get into a safe.

- When you're not using your bags, stuff them with old tops or rolled-up towels that you no longer use. This helps them keep their full shape and prevents them from creasing.

- If, like me, you have to carry the kitchen sink around with you, buy a really big, stylish tote bag with strong straps that you can just throw everything into and still look super-trendy.

- Looking for a bag that will go with everything? Choose a neutral colour in a classic shape that will last for a good few seasons and that will go with lots of different looks. It could be black, brown or beige.

- If money grew on trees, it wouldn't be a problem. Copies of top-end designer handbags are so good these days, though. If you see a copy at the fraction of the price, nab it! Check the seams and the inside to make sure it doesn't look tacky and that it's in good nick. This is a great way of tapping into a must-have trend without making yourself bankrupt.

- When choosing a tote bag, it's really important that you see how it looks when full. Before you buy it, drop your own bag into it (or your wallet and bottle of water) and you will then get an idea of how much it can hold and whether it holds its shape or not.

- If your bag is leather, clean it with leather cleaner once every three months. Wash plastic bags with a damp sponge dotted with washing-up liquid on it. And, as I've mentioned already, don't forget to hoover your bag every so often. Look after it well and it will last a good few more seasons.

- A bright-coloured bag always cheers up a plain outfit.

- Never save your 'hot off the press' handbags for special events. Do special every day so you're constantly feeling on top of the world and on top of the fashion radar too.

- If you want to get the real designer McCoy (once you've saved up the dosh), then check out the juicy deals that you can get on eBay – the prices are always slashed right down. You can also hunt down charity shops in wealthy areas where (hopefully) rich ladies will have dumped their old designer goods, which are then sold on for really low prices. Perfect for us bargain-basement babes!

BOSOM BUDDIES

I know just what it's like being the owner of a pair of raisin-like boobs and what's even worse is when all your friends' boobs are growing like rising dough while yours are just two tiny, non-existent bumps.

Try this secret weapon – fill your bras with socks or anything else spongy and filling – no one will know a thing! However, one thing that's far more attractive than having a cleavage and that's confidence! Having said that, I do have some great little tricks tucked up my sleeve to show you how to make the most of your figure.

MEASURE YOUR OWN BOOBS

When I was at school, I was so bad at maths: all those numbers and funny-looking symbols staring up at me from the paper as I stared back, confused and more than a little miffed! For me it was like learning another language. And that's why, when it came to that time in life to measure my own pair of pea-like boobs for the first time, I got it so wrong. Hurrah, I was a D cup! I couldn't quite believe my luck. Little me was a whopping size D! So off I toddled to the shops to buy my first-ever bra, but, when I got home and tried it on, I didn't look cool or pretty: I looked like I had two oversized swimming hats tied to my chest with a bit of string! So, learn your numbers and get to grips with the maths. Remember, the better you are at adding and subtracting, the better your bras will look and feel!

First, arm yourself with a soft tape. Forget working in centimetres, it's inches you need! Start off by measuring around your chest, just underneath your boobs – it's really important that the tape measure runs parallel to the floor and that both ends meet in the middle of your chest. I suggest you put it around your back and read the inches at the front. Otherwise you may end up with a bra that's one size too big or small.

Now this may sound a bit weird, but it does work. If your measurement is even, add four. For uneven numbers, add five. This gives you the band size of your bra.

To work out your cup size, measure (in inches) around the fullest part of your boobs (straight across, basically). It's important that you don't hold the tape too tightly so it squashes your boobies. Instead, let it sit firmly, but comfortably.

Now, get your mathematics head on! Once you have both measurements, subtract the band size from the last number. If the final number is 0, you are an A cup; if the final number ends up being one, you're a B cup, and if your final number ends up being a two, then lucky you, you're a whopping C cup!

If maths isn't your strong point (it was never mine), then cruise down to a big department store like John Lewis where you can ask to have your boobs professionally measured by someone who knows what they are doing!

PICK THE RIGHT BRA

- Forcing your boobs into the wrong bra is a bit like serving a burger in a hotdog bun! It doesn't work. Once they start growing, your boobs will change shape quite regularly so it's worth having them measured professionally every eight months so you know you're wearing the correct size.
- When you're in the changing room, study the back of the bra. The band should be level all the way around. If it rides up at the back and doesn't run parallel to the floor, it's probably the wrong size and won't offer any support at all. You may have to opt for a smaller band.
- There shouldn't be any baggy or excess fabric (or even space) at the top of your bra.
- The material that crosses your chest at the front of the bra should sit flat against your body.
- If you're buying an underwired bra, the wire should sit right up against your rib cage, not stand out from it.
- Straps should fit nice and snugly on your shoulders. If they dig into your flesh like a cheese wire, this is not the bra for you and you probably need to go up a size.
- If your boobs ooze out of the top of the bra, a bit like a muffin, then the cup is too small. Lucky you, you need to go up a size! A good way of checking for the muffin look is to put on a tight white T-shirt and it will soon be clear whether or not it fits properly.

HOW TO GIVE THE IMPRESSION THAT YOU'RE NOT FLAT-CHESTED – MAGIC TRICKS!

- If you're a bit of an artist at heart, this one is for you. Shade yourself a bust with your bronzer! Apply a little bronzer to your bronzing brush and swish it down your chest where you would normally see the shadow of a cleavage. If you're not sure how to do this, then get your fave weekly goss mag and check out the celebrities' boobies and their cleavage shadows.

- Wearing textures on your top, such as ruffles, pleats and heavy sequin detail or pattern will disguise the fact that you have small boobs.

- A halter-neck or off-the-shoulder-style top will put the focus on your shoulders instead.

- Never wear a bra with both padding and push-up qualities if you are flat-chested, especially if you're going to wear a tight T-shirt – your boobies will end up looking superfake! Opt for a bra that does one job or the other. T-shirt bras don't show any straps or seams and are perfect to go underneath a figure-hugging T-shirt. Ingenious!

- If you want to enhance your curves, a gel-filled bra is more natural than a padded one.

MORE TIPS FOR BRA BUYING

- Try to match the colour of your underwear as closely as you can to the colour of the outfit that you're wearing. Dark underwear under a light outfit is a cardinal sin! It's the same when wearing dark clothes: avoid wearing light undies, especially if there's a camera around to capture the moments. They will illuminate through.

- Just because you can't see your bra because it's under your top or dress doesn't mean it won't affect the overall look!

A badly fitting bra distorts the shape of all necklines on dresses and tops.

- A bra might look amazing in its own right, but it's really important that you see what it looks like with clothes on. It might be totally different and make your clothes look terrible.
- If the underwire is starting to show, it's time to say goodbye! Take the padded bits out and reuse by sewing them on to the ends of cheap hangers so your more precious and delicate clothes can hang a little more comfortably.
- Underwired bras should fit smoothly to your body, not dig in.
- If your boobs go up and down in size due to your monthly period, buy a few different sizes so you are covered at all times.
- Because of the colour and cut, different dresses need different bras. For example, if you're wearing a halter-neck dress, unsightly straps will just have the fashion police after you! Every girl needs a halter-neck bra, a backless bra, a strapless and a few regular bras in her wardrobe.
- Armed with your bra size, you might just go into a shop, grab a bra in your size and not try it on, then be surprised when you get home and it doesn't fit. Every shop varies, so you might be a 32B in one shop, but a 32C in another. Always try before you buy!
- The proper way to get yourself into a bra is to put it on the front of your body (don't do the back strap up yet), then slide the straps up in place over your shoulders, lean forward 45° and wiggle into the cups. When your boobies are firmly in place, stand up straight and do up the back clasp.
- Strapless bras are brilliant under strapless dresses or strappy smock tops. Make sure you choose the right size, though.
- If you're a sports fanatic and you already have big boobs,

you might want to invest in a sports bra, which will prevent you from getting black eyes! Shock Absorber sports bras are great.

TLC FOR BRAS

- Don't put underwired bras in the washing machine – this will cut their life in half. Handwash them instead.
- Never tumble-dry bras or put them on the radiator – it will ruin them. Instead, dry them on the line outside or hang them off the handle of a door.
- Don't just lob bras in a drawer with your knickers, socks, tights, etc. – this will cause them to tangle and catch on one another. Instead, buy one of those bra and knicker dividers that you can get in IKEA. This will keep your underwear drawer neat and tidy – and you won't be rushed into making the wrong decision when you're in a hurry and end up committing the fashion crime of choosing a black bra to go under a white top.

KNICKER MAYHEM (OR HOW TO GET OUT OF A CAR WITHOUT SHOWING YOUR PANTS TO THE WORLD!)

Thankfully, the 'no-knicker wearing' trend that Britney and Paris tried to kickstart not so long ago never took off! I mean, hardly a day goes by without Britney or Paris being snapped falling out of a car. If you want to be treated like a young lady, behave like one.

I know it can be hard at times to exit a car with grace when wearing a very short dress, but showing everyone what you had for breakfast is just too much! Here's how to exit a car with style and dignity.

- Make sure your knees are glued together from the second you move your legs to the time they hit the pavement. Use the seat that your bum's parked on to push up and out with your hands. Don't panic and grab hold of the doorframe – it's very unladylike.

- If you're wearing a micro mini, drape your cardigan, coat or shawl casually over your legs for those few all-important moments.

- While travelling, your skirt can often end up around your waist or armpits! Just before you exit the car, tug it down into place.

- If a friend offers to pick you up in a low-level sportscar, you may want to rethink your outfit – this is the worst offender for showing off your pants!

- As you exit the car, spin your body on your bum cheeks and project yourself out. This will also help keep your knees together.

- When you're out of the car, stand straight, hold yourself together and then take your first step forward.

SHOP TILL YOU DROP!

If there's one thing us girls have mastered over the years, it's shopping! To me, it's a bit like banger racing: we zoom around the shops like vehicles of destruction on a dirt track, racing against one another, trying to wreck the opposing vehicles until we've destroyed every car in sight to leave the winner (you, in this case). And like banger racing, there are really no rules when it comes to shopping in the sales, just get out there and win! Here are a few little tips to help to get you to the chequered till point… first!

- Before you hit the shops, you need a plan of action: write down exactly what you need and where you're going to go. Armed with this information, you can attack the shops like a whirlwind and scoop up lots of lovely things.

- Always set yourself a budget and stick to it when you're going shopping. An overdose will leave your piggybank feeling under the weather. It's sooo easy to get tempted by all the gorgeous bargains being waved right under your nose in the shops. Like going into a sweet shop hungry, you want the lot!

- Now put all your clothes and accessories on your bed. Literally empty out your wardrobe and drawers. Start putting outfits together, work out what's missing and therefore what you need to buy.

- Go to bed early so you can jump out, bright-eyed and bushy-tailed, way before the birdies start singing down their microphones and waking the whole world up.

- Have a good, hearty and filling breakfast before you go. Forget sugary chocolate cereals, they'll only give you a sugar rush and then you'll hit a wall of tiredness and won't have the energy to shop. Porridge! That's the magic fodder you need to scoff. It will keep your energy levels high and that sluggish feeling at bay.

- Handbag essentials are a bottle of water (it's thirsty work), healthy snacks to keep your energy levels high (banana, nuts, maybe an energy bar), mobile, pop socks (for trying on shoes), handy wipes (to clean your sticky mitts), lipgloss (looking gorge at all times is very important), mints (really refreshing when your breath kicks up a stink!), calculator (so you can add up what you've spent) and, obviously, money. Be careful when carrying dosh, though, girls – keep it hidden away, don't make it public that you are carrying money or, better still, keep it in one of those thin bum bags that go under your top – that way, no one can steal it off you and you can happily shop to your heart's content.

- To be eco-friendly, take a few plastic shopping bags with you and ask the cashier to put your new clobber in them rather than picking up a few more. This is also a great way to save money now as many shops (who are also trying to be eco-friendly and combat plastic waste) will charge you a small fee for each bag.

- Wearing clothes that are easy to pull on and off for when you want to try something on is an absolute essential. Fighting with a zillion buttons and laces will only annoy you and might result in mistake purchases.

- Equally, although kitten heels look ever so glam when you're going shopping, they just aren't practical and will kill your tootsies within the hour, which will of course result in a short shopping trip, sore feet, a miserable face and no new things! Wearing the right type of shoes is super-important if you want to zoom around, but you can still do it in style. Glam trainers, ballet shoes or tiny kitten heels that slip on and off easily will do the job just fine.

- When it comes to fashion shopping, there can be hazards. One of them is ripping your earlobes, so leave earrings at home and this will reduce the risk of you doing any damage, pulling clothes on and off.

- If you're looking for an organised store to potter about in, go in the morning when the shops first open their doors. By the afternoon, it'll be absolute chaos, with clothes chucked around the place, just like it's been freshly burgled.

- Before you buy something, have a little peek at the washing label inside. It may be dry clean only, which in the long run can end up costing more than the garment itself, especially if it's white and needs constant cleaning.

- Sometimes an item will be in the sale because it's damaged. Check carefully before you buy to see if it can be repaired. Also, if you see a mark or stain on an item of clothing and it's still full price, put your bargaining beret on and try to get a wee discount. You may not be successful, but there's no harm in trying!

- Always ask yourself this question before you buy something: if it was full price, would you still want it? If the answer's no or maybe, don't do it! And just because it's a designer item and marked down by 75%, this doesn't mean it's a bargain if you're never going to wear it.

- If you're umming and ahhing about it, chances are it doesn't look good on you, so don't get it!

- If you're going to hit the vintage shops à la Sienna Miller, there are a few simple rules to follow: don't overdo the lace, wearing it from head to toe like a Victorian; instead, mix it in with some denim for a modern take, otherwise you really will look like a cross between a doily and a dolly! If it smells really musty, there's a chance that the smell may never come out, resulting in you whiffing like a family heirloom.

- When shopping for a bikini, make sure you're wearing non-bulky underwear that won't interfere with the line of it so you get a true idea of what it will look like on you. Plus, don't remove the adhesive protective label in the bottom half of the bikini, both for hygiene reasons and because, if you do remove it, you may be charged for the item even if you decide you don't really want it.

- It's really important that you do a bit of jumping around in a bikini to see how it sits on your body. If it disappears right up your bottom after only a couple of jumps, it's not for you. You won't want to be playing volleyball on the beach with half your bum on show, will you?

- If you're shopping for a winter coat and it's the end of the summer and baking hot, don't try it on over your summer dress – you need a sweater. There's no point in trying it on without bulk only to discover that it doesn't fit when the harsh weather kicks in and you need to layer up.

- When shopping for a little glitzy disco-diva number, it's worth putting on a little lipgloss and mascara to make you feel glam. A blotchy, greasy face will only put you off, whatever you try on.

- It's really important that you take a walk around the store to get an idea of how new shoes feel. Ask yourself, do they pinch, make my legs look unflattering or do they force me to change my posture? If the answer to any of these is yes, don't buy them.

- When buying a dress, let's say it's for your end-of-year ball or disco, where you know you will have to stand, sit and dance in it all night long, it's worth doing all those activities in the shop so you know it does what it says on the label. If it feels uncomfortable at any time or ruches up when you sit down, don't get it. It's not going to get any better and it will ruin your night!

- A hot chocolate break is an absolute must when you're out shopping and great for recharging the batteries.

- Some girls don't mind communal changing rooms but it can be the worst nightmare for others. Just in case you have to try your clothes on in a communal changing room, make sure you wear underwear that you don't mind everybody seeing.

- If you're going out to buy a dress, wear the underwear that you think you will wear with it and take the right heels so you get the whole feeling of it.

- Never take your brother or boyfriend shopping. Trust me, they'll only sit there huffing and puffing, looking at their watches and wishing they were anywhere but with you, telling you everything looks good just so they can get you out of the shop as quickly as possible. Take a best girlfriend with a good eye for fashion, or buy it by yourself, take it home and then get a second opinion. If it's not right, get a refund (check the store's policy before you buy). You may need to take your mum if she's paying for it or if she's the one getting the refund.

- If you see an item of clothing that you can't live without, but it doesn't fit, then ask the shop assistant whether they have an in-house seamstress who could alter it to fit you. Otherwise, take it to the local dry cleaners where they usually do alterations, or if your mum is a dab hand on the sewing machine then you can always ask her nicely, of course.

- An overcoat is a very hard thing to alter (unlike a dress or a pair of trousers), so, if it doesn't look totally amazing the first time you try it on, don't even think about it!

- Never go shopping with greasy, chip-pan-textured hair – no matter how lovely the outfit, this will always make you feel ugly.

- If you're looking to buy a pair of those lovely stretchy long boots that literally are like a second skin, don't go out wearing your jeans – they won't go over the top properly for an honest fit. Wear a skirt or dress instead.

- Wait until the end of the sales to grab some seriously good, bottom-of-the-barrel bargains. In these credit crunch times, shops are literally giving the stuff away.

- And finally, remember that one of the best things about shopping, other than stocking up your wardrobe with some yummy new additions, is that all that hotfooting it around is actually quite good exercise for you and a chance to get together with your mates!

FASHION FORWARD

Hunting down that killer wardrobe isn't about splashing the cash, it's about training your fashion-savvy eye to pick and choose clothes that make you feel and look good so you stamp your own personality without breaking the bank.

A truly stylish girl knows that fashion is all about mixing high street and designer with a hint of vintage for a truly eclectic mix. It's not about having a mountain of clothes wedged in your straining wardrobe that cost the earth, it's about being resourceful and having a streamlined set of garments that make you look your best for every occasion, expected or not.

So the bottom line is – you don't need to be minted to look stylish! A small budget often brings creativity to the table, whereas lots of cash may bring cheap and costly mistakes to your closet. I'm sure I've heard Paris Hilton suggesting that it takes loads of cash to look this cheap! I rest my case!

DARE TO LOOK DIFFERENT

- If you're not sure how you look in something, then get a friend to take a picture of you from every angle wearing that item. Load it up on to your computer and check it out. Photographs can really help us to see what we look like from all angles.
- Have different pairs of jeans for when you wear both high heels and flats. We've all naughtily worn our favourite jeans with a pair of pumps, only to wake up the next day and see that we've scuffed the bottom of the fabric. Jeans for flats should always be shorter than those worn with your high heels.
- If you've been invited to a really funky party and you've blown your allowance for the month, but want to look different, then ask your mum to blow-dry your hair, maybe

put some curlers in, etc. I swear you'll feel gorgeous and fab, like you're wearing a new frock anyway.

- I absolutely love vintage or secondhand shops as you can always find really stunning and unusual pieces. When you're having a good old hunt around these boutique places just be sure not to buy any clothing that has any signs of rotting, irreparable lining or moth-holes. Vintage shops can be more expensive, but some high-street stores like Topshop have great vintage sections at a fraction of the price. Car boot sales, good charity shops and eBay are also great places to find delectable little delights.

- To make a cheap shirt look unique and expensive, remove the buttons and sew on some funkier ones.

- I know the fashion magazines ALWAYS say black is back, but black truly is a good friend to have hanging around in your wardrobe. It's such a great backdrop to colours: for instance, wearing acid yellow and black looks sharp, and a floral pattern looks so good on a black background, while metallics and white are amazing. Head-to-toe black can also make you look quite pale and pasty too as it may drain the colour from your complexion. Just make sure you add a zest of colour around your face to liven things up a bit. Throughout the whole of my school life, I was always the shortest in class, but I made sure I never looked it. You see, I had a little trick that kind of stretched me out and that gave the impression that I was taller than I really was. I would wear my hair up in a really high ponytail and I used to wear vertical stripes.

- There's nothing I enjoy more than having a good old flick through a fashion magazine to catch up on all of the celeb gossip and to see who's wearing what. To me they're a bit like a bible, really! You can learn so much, from fashion to beauty to what to do about your love life. If you're in a rut and don't know where or how to start building a new wardrobe or how to put outfits together, check out the magazines and see which celeb's wardrobe you admire, then recreate elements of her image to get your own look.

- To give a smart-looking dress a bit of cheeky chick edge, how about throwing on a pair of biker boots or maybe wearing some fab strong-coloured lippy, or even funking your hair up a bit?

- Have a flick through *Teen Vogue* and translate the runway looks into something that you could genuinely wear for those wannabe 'stick-it-all-together' style gurus.

- If you feel uncomfortable in what you're wearing and you're constantly tugging away at your clothes to try to sort them out, it will come across in your personality and you'll end up looking uncomfortable and unconfident.

- Some trends can be really strong in character. If this is the case and you don't feel confident enough to carry them, how about just picking out a few elements and mixing them in with what you're already comfortable with? Accessories are always a good place to start.

- Colour is a very powerful tool. It has the ability to make us look tall, short, happy, sad, big, small, etc., so make sure you choose wisely. Just because it looks good on your best friend, it doesn't mean it's going to work on you. If you don't know where to start, begin with a neutral palette (beige, black, brown, white, blue) and add a touch of colour at a time. Hold the colour up to your face and see how it reacts against your skin. You soon see which colours make you look best.

- If you have got tiny boobies then you can definitely get away without having to wear a bra with certain dresses such as a backless style.

- Bit of a Sweaty Betty? You're better off wearing cotton clothes – they are great at absorbing sweat. Avoid Lycra at all costs unless you like that feeling of glued-on sticky clothes.

- Fashion-wise, September can be so annoying! One moment it's glorious sunshine and you're tottering about the place, Sienna Miller style, in your floaty summer dress with a fabulous hat and gorgeous scrummy sandals and then, seconds later, the skies have gone black, the heavens open up. The best way to combat the problem is to leave the house wearing a few thin layers. If it's cold, you can wear them all and, if it's hot, remove some of them, one at a time.

- My Saturdays are usually taken up with going to different markets. I love them because they're full of great things at really cheap prices that I can take home and customise.

- Car boot sales are fantastic – you take very little money with you, yet you come home with masses of stuff! If you're looking to give your bedroom a makeover, you'll find plenty here plus lots of lovely fashion accessories, etc.

- It's a bit of an understatement to say that a pair of jeans is one of the most important items any girl should have in her wardrobe. If you don't have a decent pair, get one now! Jeans resist dirt, they don't wrinkle easily, they can be dressed up (with sparkly jewellery and heavenly heels) or dressed down (flat pumps and a cute sweater, or rolled up with flip-flops for the summer months) and they go with every colour and texture under the sun.

- If you're in the mood to experiment and feel like mixing two trends together, go ahead – as long as they work together and complement each other. Anything other than that and you'll look like you're wearing your whole wardrobe out at once, as if you've been pre-decorated in time for Christmas!

- If you like to experiment with wild and wacky clothes and

accessories, best to do this at home rather than scaring the neighbours! Finding your personal style and creating new looks is such fun. Once you have found your individual look, flaunt it with pride.

- You might be wearing the coolest dress in town but, if you're all hunched over and dragging your feet around like a pair of brooms, this will make your outfit look drab and ill-fitting. If your posture is straight and statuesque (head up, bum in, boobies out, standing tall, etc.), your clothes will automatically shine. When you look confident, your outfit will seem more expensive and you'll be fashion fabulous 24/7. The following might sound a bit crazy but it's a great way to build confidence if you don't feel it: practise on the white-haired brigade! Yep, the grannies! If you are near a door and granny wants to pass through it, open the door and say, 'After you.' Your politeness should trigger a positive reaction from her (unless she's an ungrateful old misery guts!), plus it forces you to strike up a conversation with someone new. Once you have practised on a handful of grannies, use this new-found skill and adapt it for when you have to walk into a room full of new people where you don't know anyone. I think you will really notice how helpful this exercise can be.

- The nautical style is so much fun. Just for your knowledge, the wider or thicker the stripe, the more casual the look will be, and the thinner the stripe, the more formal it is.

- Long coats can look so elegant, but, if you're really short, opt for a three-quarter length instead or you'll be forever picking it up off the floor and will look like a midget!

- If you plan to wear something pretty crazy looking, it's a good idea to mix and match it with an item that's a little more classic.

- Always give the impression of having just thrown it

together rather than looking as if you've spent the best part of the day parked up in front of your bedroom mirror. It's far cooler to be laidback than to look as if you've tried too hard.

● Variety is the spice of fashion life… and everything else, come to think of it!

YOUR SAFETY NET

Really cheap clothing is, I think, very similar to fast food. You buy it, wear it once or twice, then you lob it. I mean, how wasteful is that? Plus, it's bad news for those already-brimming landfill sites that are ruining beautiful countryside. I'm sure your mum will agree that it's worth spending a little more money on a good classic item, such as a winter coat, that you know you will wear a lot. Here are some more useful tips.

● If you want to get value for money and for your clothes to be as versatile as possible, go for colours and fabrics that work with the rest of your wardrobe. Start off with neutral colours, such as beige, black, white and brown, then build colour on to and around these.

● Remember, high-maintenance clothes are like high-maintenance friends – they need a lot of attention and looking after, for example, dry-clean-only clothes! Always check the washing label before you purchase an item. Having to dry clean something after every wearing can end up being very costly.

● There are two types of chicks, those who follow fashion religiously and buy every new must-have item that moves, with the knowledge that they will most definitely be out of fashion in six months because the new season has arrived, and then there are those who like to dip in and out of trends, and are more likely to go for neutral and classic clothes that won't date too quickly. I myself fall into the latter – I like to dip in and out of fashion like a yo-yo, enjoying it, but not following it like it's a matter of life or death.

- A tuxedo blazer is like a very tailored version of a school blazer and it's a huge hit with our favourite fashion-savvy celebs. It looks hot with jeans, cute short floral mini dresses and denim shorts. If you want to funk it up a little bit more, attach a really cool badge to the lapel.

- When buying a winter coat, it's worth spending a little bit more so you get a good few years out of it. Colourwise, you're better opting for black, beige, navy and brown which will go with most of your existing wardrobe. Avoid high-fashion details that will date by next season, too.

- Visiting really good vintage shops can be a great way to add zest to your capsule wardrobe, plus you'll be investing in something that's unusual and likely to be a quality, even designer label.

- Whether you're off to the beach or a BBQ, or simply enjoying the sun, summer dresses are made for having fun in. For this reason, don't spend a fortune on your frocks or you'll always be worrying about getting something on them and never feel totally relaxed.

- Because your shoes get a lot of wear and tear, you're better off spending more on them and less on your clothes. Plus, if you're wearing good shoes, everyone will assume that your clothes are equally pricey, too.

- Whether it's money you've earned yourself from a Saturday job or if you've saved up the cash from babysitting – or maybe you're going halves with your mum and dad, it's wise to set a budget in advance and sticking to it is a good way to stop yourself spending too much. You might also want to think ahead and ask for certain items, such as a striking watch, for your birthday or Christmas. But what should you be investing in, and where can you make savings? Here's a list of the items I recommend you have in your wardrobe. If you choose wisely, the pricier ones should last you a good few years, while the cheaper items can be changed more frequently before they start to look shabby.

What to Spend On
- Good shoes – everyday shoes, trainers, ballet pumps, ankle boots
- Winter overcoat – an absolute staple in winter
- Jacket – a smart one. Good for interviews, etc.
- Daytime handbag that is able to fit your whole life in.
- Trousers – smart black, navy or beige. Great for a potential job interview.
- Smart sweaters in a range of colours and styles
- Fitted blazer
- A striking watch
- Jeans – a fabulously well-cut pair that goes from day to night easily

Where to Save
- Funky accessories such as earrings, bracelets, necklaces, scarves, belts and rings, etc.
- T-shirts in all colours
- Cheap rock and roll Ts that you can cut up and customise
- Jeans – cheapish ones that again can be dyed, cut up and customised
- Gorgeous summer dresses
- Cardigans
- Glitzy party bag

- Bras and knickers (check out the high street!)
- Squidgy sweaters for Sundays and slobbing around

- Don't go shopping when you're in a bad mood, in a hurry or maybe you have PMT. You'll make all sorts of shopping mistakes because you'll be impulse buying without really thinking... And when you get home, you'll be in such a grump because your wardrobe will be bursting at the seams with loads of things you don't want to wear.
- No one ever keeps this next tip up for long, but it does work! Colour-code your wardrobe. It will make your life a lot easier when you next decide what to wear. Depending on your mood, you will naturally gravitate towards the right colour and it will save you time in the morning when you're looking for inspiration.
- If you and the weather need a bit of cheering up, then wear yellow and bring some sunshine into your life.
- My brown, yellow and beige get-up was officially the worst-looking school uniform in the universe. It was hideous! Thankfully, I was born with a creative gene ... I used my hair as the decoy to attract attention away from what I was wearing. You see, your hair can have a huge impact on your outfit. By putting it up into a variety of fashion forward hair-dos such as a J-Lo slicked-back ponytail, a Sienna Miller boho look or maybe a Vanessa Hudgens luscious locks number, you can radically transform a look. Depending on how strict your school is about your uniform, how about ditching the clumpy frumpy shoes and trading them in for some really cool ones? You can also chuck the minging school satchel to the back of the wardrobe and switch it for a really hip (but still practical) handbag! And don't forget some sparkly hair clips to jazz up your crowning glory!

- If you're hitting the coffee shops with the girls after school but want to do it in a stylish, way then you need a few stylish must-haves stashed away in your school bag – Nicole Richie sunnies, an Alexa Chung chequered scarf, some sparkly hair clips, some cool key rings to hang off your bag and a handful of funky bracelets. Ditch the tie, undo the top button of your shirt and, lastly, don't forget the most important accessory of all – a whopping, confident smile.

- What to wear at your school disco. This is your time to put some razzle dazzle into the party and show 'em who's the queen of the dancefloor – both by cutting some seriously cool dance shapes, Rihanna-style, and in the fashion department. Firstly, anything sparkly is a must. Bright, colourful eye make-up and outrageous hair-dos are the way forward if you want to get noticed. Showing off too much flesh all at once is a HUGE no-no. The general rule is – either show off a bit of flesh on the bottom (ie wear a mini) and stay more covered on the top, or show a wee bit of flesh on the top (cute little strappy top) and cover on the bottom (a pair of jeans for instance). If you want to wear a dress that stands out, then try a sixties-style mini dress with huge hoop earrings! Seriously hot! If you want to be the last standing on the dancefloor, then leave high heels at home and instead opt for a pair of sharp-looking kitten heels.

FAST FIXES FOR FASHION EMERGENCIES

We've all done it, haven't we – sat in somebody else's chewing gum? Other than having to prise it off, the worst thing is that you've probably been walking around all day like that, looking like a right goof! And then of course there's the heel problem. You know, the one where your heel decides to break at the most inconvenient of times when you are either out on a date and trying to impress potential new boyfriend material, or on your way to the most important job or college interview of your whole life, where making a really good first impression really counts, and turning up with both shoes intact is always a better move than turning up with one. There's no immediate solution, so what do you do? Hobble around like you've got one leg shorter than the other, or brazen it out? Rather than getting your knickers in a twist, I say style it out every time by following my tips and no one will notice!

- If you've managed to get chewing gum stuck to your clothes, fear not, Lazy Princesses! With luck, you'll be wearing a jumper or a cardigan, so tie it around your waist. When you get home, pop your trousers or skirt in an old plastic bag and stick it in the freezer for a few hours. With an everyday knife (not a super-sharp carver), slowly pick it all off. If it happens when you're out in a cool café with your friends, order a glass of water with ice. When it arrives, dunk your hand in there, grab an ice cube and suck the liquid off it. Now go to the bathroom and rub the ice cube on the offending area until it becomes cold and hard, then pick it off.
- If you love animals, but you also like wearing velvet, I'm sure you'll know what I mean by 'hairy velvet'! Because I grew up surrounded by cats, dogs, horses and chickens, there were always stray animal hairs kicking around the place and I remember my mum wrapping sticky tape around her hands, three or four times, and then grooming herself as if she was grooming one of the horses. You can do the same when you wear velvet or any other hair-attracting fabric.
- Tights are expensive and ladder all the time. If you ladder your tights, stick a thin layer of clear nail varnish on the

ladder (keep some in your bag) and this will prevent the run from getting any worse.

- If the heel on your shoe snaps off, the worst thing you could do is look like a rabbit caught in the headlights. Style it out! So, if someone stops and quizzes you about your strange, one-heeled look, look really condescending and tell them they obviously don't get fashion. If you say it with confidence they will believe you, and anyway you never know you may set off a new trend. Watch out, Mary-Kate and Ashley Olsen!

- If you are one of those chicks who always loses her coat or bag out and about or at school, write your name and number (or your mum's work number or one that she doesn't mind being given out) on to a little piece of card and pop it somewhere it can easily be spotted (stick a small label on your umbrella). Whoever finds it will be able to ring your mum so you can go and collect it (don't go on your own to pick it up though, take your mum or dad, unless of course you know the person well).

- Deodorant marks are just as bad as big old sweat patches. To get rid of those nasty, ghostly marks, just dampen a white towel or flannel with warm water and dab until it's gone. You can also buy deodorants that are specially designed so they don't leave marks in the first place.

- Another good way to banish sweaty marks is to get a breakfast bowl or a Tupperware box, pop some hot water (about 1.5 pints) into it, along with three teaspoons of salt. Give it a good mix, dunk a T-towel or sponge into it and dab it on to the chalky patch until it's all gone.

- Another good way to get rid of sweaty patches is to take the item off, spritz it with some clear vinegar, then pop into a bowl with a mixture of water and two aspirins (ask your mum before taking the aspirins). Now twizzle it with your finger and let the magic take place.

- You can, of course, buy sweat pads, which you attach to the armpit section of your clothes and they absorb all of the sweat.
- Thin sanitary towels can also be stuck to the armpits of your blazer and they will absorb all the sweat so you won't get sweaty patches on the outside of your jacket. Just be careful when you take off your jacket, though. I'm not sure how cool it would make you look if two sodden sweaty sanitary towels suddenly came flying out of your jacket. Nice!
- If you're out with your friends and you're really hot, quickly run into the bathroom and stuff lots of loo roll under each armpit to soak up the excess sweat, then dunk the underside of your wrists underneath running cold water. This will quickly bring your temperature down and reduce your sweating.
- So, you're at the school disco and the cool dress that everyone has been ooh-ing and ahh-ing over decides to fall apart. Yep, the hem has gone AWOL. Rather than leaving the party early with an upside-down smile, put it back in place with double-sided sticky tape (keep a mini-roll in your bag for emergencies or ask if you can raid the cupboard in the art department). This will last until you can get it properly mended.
- One of the handles breaking on your heavenly handbag can be very upsetting, I know, but all you have to do is tuck both handles in and carry it like a big clutch instead.
- If your badly behaved ballpoint has leaked ink all over your fave top, don't throw it away! Instead, dab some washing-up liquid on to the ink area and gently scrape away at it. Rinse and then repeat until it all comes out. As a last resort, blob more ink on to it so that it looks as if it's meant to be like that!

- Getting ready to go out is sooooo much fun, especially when you do it with your friends, but don't just head dive into your frock or top – you'll only end up getting make-up all over it! Instead, put a silk handkerchief or a T-towel over your face and slip your dress/top over your head to prevent make-up getting on your clothes. If, despite this, you do manage to get make-up on it, don't panic and drown the garment in water to get rid of the stain because the mark will just get bigger and can even spread. Only ever use a tiny bit of warm water on a white cloth to remove a mark. Or use a little bit of washing-up liquid as a last resort.

- If the hem on your trousers comes down, then take it down totally on both legs, iron over the crease and wear higher shoes. Or tide yourself over by securing it with some double-sided tape.

- I'm afraid it's impossible to reverse the colour if you get bleach on a top or trousers. Rather than getting upset, use this mistake to your advantage. Put some rubber gloves on and splash a bit more bleach artistically and your top will no longer look like a mistake, but a unique one-off piece.

Cleo from Cleopatra - *The Girl Band*

Getting sweaty smells and stains out of clothes can be tough and the quicker you tend to them the better. Hand wash the affected area in cold water or rinse hard. If the stain is dried, leave it to soak for ten minutes. The stain or odour should be gone, or at least very faint, leaving you to wash as normal

- If you've been good and gone for a swim at the local swimming pool, rather than waiting until you get home to chuck your swimsuit in the washing machine, give it a little rinse at the sports centre and this will prevent the chlorine from discolouring it. The same applies when you have been at the beach for the day. Make sure you rinse out the salt.

Richard Ward – Hairdresser to the Stars

THE SKIN-TONE TEST

To find out your skin tone, sit in front of a mirror in natural daylight. Ensure you are wearing no make-up (or fake tan) and scrape your hair back, preferably in a towel or turban. Take two separate pieces of fabric – a scarf, or item of clothing is good. Take one warm-toned colour (a peach or orange is good) and one cool-toned (a lilac or fuchsia is the most obvious). Wrap the fabric around your face and neck and then swap. One colour will automatically make your eyes sparkle and your skin look vibrant. One will flatten and deaden your skin, making it look sallow. If still unsure, try just using lipstick. Using the colour tones above, apply the lilac/pink tone first then remove it and apply a warm, golden tone. You will soon instantly see which colour family you belong to.

Famous warm people: Nicole Kidman, Kate Winslet, Charlize Theron, Jennifer Aniston

Famous cool people: Elizabeth Hurley, Angelina Jolie, Eva Longoria, Heidi Klum

BRIGHT SPARK

We've all got our favourite colours, haven't we? Some make us look tanned and toned, others make us appear healthy and happy, while some can make us seem ill! Colours have the amazing power to make us look happy or sad, glisten or glum, stumpy or tall, fat or thin, so follow my colour guidelines, understand the category into which you fall and look forever like a golden gorge-pants!

- First things first, rummage through your wardrobe and see which items you love and wear the most, and the ones you're always complimented on. Don't worry about shape, just look for shades that suit the colours in your complexion. Stand in front of a mirror that faces lots of daylight. If the colour suits you, you will look healthy, rosy, gorgeous and alive and, if it doesn't work, you'll appear dull and drained; it may even highlight how tired you look.
- When you're in the shop, find a mirror in daylight. Hold the item you like up against your face and see what it does to your complexion. See if you notice yourself first or the colour. If it's the colour, this may be the wrong shade for you. Often a garment can look amazing on the hanger, but, when you hold it up against your face, it can look different altogether.
- Whatever colour you go for, it should always harmonise, not clash, with your skin tone, eye colour and hair colour.
- The right colours for you will make you look prettier, healthier and even thinner, plus your complexion will seem flawless.

So what type are you? Read on!

- Blonde babes look good in pinks, zesty yellows, coral, blacks, green and whites, but try to avoid blacks and whites if you have really pale skin – they will wash out any colour you may have.
- Rebellious redheads and gorgeous ginger girls look great in greens, teals and hot gold. Pink is a no-no.
- Beautiful brunettes can go for pretty much every colour, from hot oranges and zesty yellows to beiges, browns, reds, pinks and bright neons. Pastels are probably the colours to avoid. Strong all the way, honeys!
- Babe-alish black hair looks good in yellows, pinks, blacks, blues and gold.

Now, here's my guide to the colours themselves and how they work for you.

- Pink: The girliest of the bunch! Don't do a Miss Piggy, though, and wear too much of it in one outfit.
- Black: This can look super-hot, or like the walking dead! Use bright accessories around your face to stop it from draining your healthy glow.
- Orange: One of summer's hot favourites, plus an autumn essential. It adds zest to any outfit. Rusty metal, tango or a roaring fire orange, this one will make sure you won't melt into the background. Maybe stay clear if you have a pink skin tone or you're a little sunburned, though. It may end up clashing and you could look like a glowing beacon!
- Green: All you eco chicks out there, this earthy colour makes you look friendly and fresh! The trick here is not to wear green from head to toe so you look like an elf hiding in a bush, but just enough to appear effortlessly cool and stylish.
- Blue: A colour that will never go out of fashion, rather like black. In summer it looks refreshing with white and during

the winter it's slick with purples. Wearing blue with black isn't the most flattering combo, I must admit. Blue can be worn on the sports field or to a glitzy party.

- Brown: Get creative and make this colour work for you! Don't think about school uniforms, it's chocolate, frothy cappuccinos and tasty nutmegs. If brown isn't for you, then wear a brown belt instead. It looks great with other earthy colours such as greens and greys.

- Beige: The sophisticated alternative to white and a lot more flattering, to be honest. It's the colour that all of the other shades just love as it's chilled out and not attention grabbing. Never wear it from head to toe unless you want to look like a giant stick of French bread or kill it off with black shoes! Keep them light instead.

- Red: You'll sizzle, sizzle when you wear this and get noticed. Mix it in with fuchsia and hot pinks to keep the look really edgy.

- White: Fresh, fabulous and very high maintenance. There are so many shades around, from creamy to very cold. Find a shade that suits your skin tone.

- Purple: The professional party-goer's favourite. It looks so hot with over-the-top silver or gold bling. Team this luxurious regal colour with bright yellows, burgundy, a touch of fuchsia pink or olive green.

- Grey: One of the ultimate and most stylish colours; also one of the best foundations to showcase other colours such as yellows, purples and pinks. It's a daytime colour really, but can look amazing at night. Wearing grey with black will drain the colour from your face, though.

- Yellow: You know when this colour comes out of your wardrobe that spring has arrived! If you're not comfortable wearing yellow, add a hint of it with a handbag or a belt.

- Metallics: A chick just can't get enough of them! Tarnished gold and silver or bright gold and silver add such impact to any outfit. Plus, there's a tone to suit everybody out there.

FASHION MISTAKES THAT SHOULD REALLY BE EXTINCT

It's obvious some people don't own a mirror or haven't heard of one at that, otherwise they wouldn't leave the house looking like they got dressed in the dark. For instance, so many chicks parade down the street with their tacky thongs on show, looking like a stuffed sausage because their tops are too tight or waddling like a penguin because their belt is strangled around their knees in an attempt to hold up their rapper-style baggy trousers!

Although fashion trends come and go with every season, some things are always wrong. If you're going to be the one who commits a crime against fashion, I sincerely hope you have a nice friend who will point it out to you so you don't make the same mistake again! Here's what to avoid:

- Toilet paper on the end of your foot.
- Attaching your mobile to the belt on your trousers. So nerdy!
- Wearing dark underwear under light clothing – it just looks tacky.
- Bum cleavage is so wrong!
- Boys' Y-fronts on show – throw them out now! I have no idea why girls wear them – they just look like you're wearing manky old dishcloths.
- There's only one person who can get away with wearing white socks with dark sandals and that's the amazing Michael Jackson. Everyone else should keep away from this look.

- VPL (Visible Panty Line) – it's amazing how many gals spend hours deciding what to wear when they're going out only to go and neglect their underwear. You can't just wear anything! Each outfit requires different undies.

- Leather worn head to toe is fine if you're a biker and actually have a bike, but, other than that, it's a huge no-no!

- Don't wear light, coloured clothing under dark clothing. Believe it or not, we can still see it!

- Denim worn head to toe was cool back in the 1970s, but it certainly isn't now.

- Socks and sandals with summer shorts: Trust me, it's not a good combo! You might have seen your dad sporting this look, but really this doesn't make it OK to do so.

- Christmas jumpers with reindeers and mince pies, etc. on them should be thrown out with the discarded wrapping paper.

- Low-rise jeans with a flabby belly on show only looks like you're wearing a flesh apron as it hangs over the top of your trousers. Cover it up or do some sit-ups!

- Baggy trousers where the crotch is worn down around the ankles: If you're not a gang member, don't dress like one.

- Wearing red jeans and a red T-shirt together makes you look like a giant sweet red pepper.

- Bum bags: Whoever came up with this invention should be sent to prison for the worst fashion crime ever!

- Wearing too many patterns at once: Looking like you're one big wallpaper sample board only appeals to those looking for inspiration for decorating their living rooms, other than that, it's just too much.

BIKINI BABE OR BEACH BUM?

When the time of year is ripe and that juicy golden beach beckons you to its waters, you know it's time to pack the Barbie-sized beach bag with your effortlessly chic-kini and kaftan, gather the gals and hit the sandy plains. But don't leave your stylish side at home, here's how to look like a trendy Wendy on the cheap and chic!

What to Take

- Huge WAG-style sunglasses – to spy on the boys from behind your magazine!
- Good trash to read – all the weekly gossip magazines or a juicy hot book
- A seriously stylish straw hat that folds up and squishes down easily
- Your iPod, complete with rocking tunes
- Boho sandals to totter about in
- Plastic sandals so that you can walk on the rocks without cutting your tootsies
- Beach towel
- Snacks
- Sun cream – a strong one to keep those harmful rays from burning your skin
- A cool and multipurpose kaftan or sarong that can be used to change behind, to look stylish and cool at the café bar, to hide a wobbly white bum and also to protect you from the sun when it gets too fierce
- Some cash to buy a round of ice creams!

Before you hit the beach, it's time to pick a bikini! Read through my rundown to find the bikini or swimsuit that best suits your shape.

Short Body

- If your body looks like it's been chopped in half and you want to give the illusion that it's longer than it is, wear thin vertical stripes. Or wear a vertical-striped swimming costume with high-cut sides.

Long Body

- If your body is too long and you want to shorten it, wear horizontal stripes. You can also go for a two-piece bikini, where the top half is an off-the-shoulder-style crop top. The gap that the two-piece creates will break up your long torso.
- A two-piece bikini is always more flattering than a one-piece swimming costume because the flesh on show breaks up the expanse of material, therefore the length of your body. Bold prints or patterns will also disguise a long body.

Flabby Tummy

- Invest in a double-layered structured bikini to hold everything in the right place. Wearing a dark colour (brown, black or maybe red) with a small print is great for disguising lumps and bumps. This will make you look much more slender.
- A swimming costume with ruching on one side will totally disguise the rolls. You could also wear a swimming costume with a bold print. Again, this will disguise the lumps you don't want anyone else to see.

Flat-chested

- Choose a bikini with a bit of padding, not too much though or it will only look as if you're carrying a pair of foam pads around with you. Crochet and ruffled tops are great for disguising non-existent boobs, while halter-necks are better than a regular bra-strap shape and will make the most of your figure.

- To make small boobies look bigger in a bikini, wear a light-coloured, patterned halter top with dark bottoms.

Large Bust

- Thin spaghetti straps just won't do the job properly and your boobs will dance all around the place. Consider trying a halter-neck style, which will give them all the support that they need. Underwired cups will also give support.
- Rather than wearing a bikini top that's a completely different colour to the bottoms, go for a matching two-piece to balance out your body shape. If you want to go for a two-piece that doesn't match in colour, try a top in a dark colour and bottoms in a lighter shade. Wearing a top that's bright in colour will make your baps shine like beacons, therefore drawing a lot of attention to that area.
- Look for bikinis that are sold as separates so that, if you have a small bottom and a big top, you can choose them separately (cup size for the top and clothes size for the bottom).

Big Bottom

- Opt for a bikini shape that isn't too small or it will disappear between your bum cheeks! Also, one that isn't too big. Trying to cover a larger derrière with lots of fabric only makes it look big. Look for a style that covers the bare essentials generously and flatters your bum shape too.
- Avoid wearing white. The most flattering bikini bottom should have full sides, not ties or strings, and double-layered material. A sarong will make you feel more comfortable,

especially if you are tottering up to the beachside café for lunch or going for a stroll.

- Some chicks mistakenly believe that, by stretching a huge piece of fabric over their bottoms, they can reduce the size of it. Covering your bum with a vast amount of fabric only makes it look bigger. Look for a shape that draws the eye up your figure.
- A wide waistband on the bottom half helps give a wobbly tum a little bit of support. Patterns in a small, dark print work well, too.
- Apply a layer of fake tan before you hit the beach – it will always look more flattering.
- Wear a strapless swimming costume and then the focus will be on your shoulders, not your bum.

Short Stubby Legs
- Go for a bikini with a high cut – it will make your legs appear longer.
- Chilled-out wedges are a girl's best friend and magically make your short stumps instantly look streamlined and much longer.
- A tie-side bottom will help to stretch out those stumps. Graduating colours also elongate short legs.

Broad shoulders
- Halter-neck styles help to make your shoulders appear less broad.

No Waist
- Create one with a belted swimming costume or buy a super-cool costume with trendy cutouts around the waist area to give the illusion of curves.

- Try a bikini with a belt on the bottom half or maybe even a cute little bow on the waist.

PERFECT PACKING

Going on holiday can actually be quite stressful at times so much so that it's a wonder there are any trees left in this world – the amount of paper lists us girls make in the run-up is quite unbelievable. Do you need a straw or floppy hat with that outfit? Red or orange nail polish with a floral frock or big feather earrings to go with the Russian gypsy boots? Never-ending, isn't it? Then, just when you think you've nailed a clever capsule wardrobe for a week's holiday that will cover all occasions from day to night, from glam to sporty, etc., you find yourself jumping up and down on your poor old suitcase like it's a trampoline, trying to shut it!

If you're guilty of overpacking and literally take your wardrobe with you on holiday, here's the best way to pack like a pro!

- Make a list of everything that you need to take, from plugs and passport to sarong and sizzling lipgloss.
- Being a successful packer is not an easy job. Be tough on yourself: don't start adding extras just in case. If it's not on the list, it's not coming with you!
- Hard case suitcases are great for protecting your clothes from outside water damage. Also, if you're carrying breakables, then the hard case at least gives them a better chance of surviving the journey.
- So that you can identify your suitcase from all the other identical ones on the luggage carousel at the airport, tie a bit of distinctive ribbon around it. I tie a bit of outrageous-looking red and white spotted ribbon around one of my handles. It really works!

- Choose the right suitcase: one that's light, but roomy. These days there are luggage weight restrictions – if your bag is too heavy, then you (or your parents) will have to pay excess. Make sure someone in your family has checked online beforehand.
- If you have limited space in your suitcase but want to take loads of clothes with you, buy some of those brilliant vacuum bags. All you have to do is pop your clothes in the bags, zip them up and, using a vacuum cleaner, suck out all the air until everything has shrunk to midget size.
- Remember, the less you take, the more shopping you can do!
- Arrange your shoes in pairs, heel to toe and then wrap them in old plastic bags. Not only will this ensure they stay together as a pair for optimum space saving but it will also prevent them from dirtying your clothes during the journey. You may want to stuff your shoes (and any handbags) with your knickers and socks just so that they hold their shape while travelling.
- Put heavy stuff, like shoes and your wash bag, at the bottom of the case so they don't squash your clothes.
- Pop your cleansers and other skincare items into little sandwich bags and seal them up to avoid leakages.
- To save on suitcase weight, buy presents for the person who has invited you in the country you are visiting, rather than lugging lots of stuff to the other side of the world.
- Take waterproof mascara with you if you're going near the beach. Two black lines streaming down your face isn't a cool look!
- Don't stuff clothes into your suitcase days before you're due to leave. I know it's good to be organised, but you will only arrive on your holiday with creased clothes! Lay them

out on your bed or hang them on the side of your wardrobe, then pop them in at the last minute.

- Linen looks great, but it's a nightmare for creasing up, which makes it look really scruffy. Go for fabrics that spring back into shape within seconds – unless you want to be tied to the iron all week!

- Pack items of clothing that mix and match in two or three different ways. This will limit the amount you have to take and you'll get so much more wear out of each item.

- Put tweezers, liquids, razors or any other sharp objects into your suitcase – you won't be allowed to take them in your hand luggage. If you forget to put them in your case, they'll be confiscated before your security check.

- Offer to help mum and dad out by doing some household chores for them – for a small wage, of course! The money can go towards buying new and exciting holiday nick-nacks.

- If you're taking a beach bag with you, use this as your hand luggage. Remember, no liquids (over 100ml – and no more than 1 litre over all) or sharp objects may be taken in your hand luggage.

- If you're on a long-haul flight, don't forget to take your mini toothpaste and brush, a pair of pyjamas, a clean pair of knickers, some face wipes to freshen up before you land and fresh fruit to cleanse your dry mouth.

- Take a light rain mac, one that can be squished up into a neat little package. You never know when the heavens might decide to open!

- If you're taking your fave big squidgy sweater, wear it on the plane to save valuable space in your suitcase.

- Decant your shampoo, conditioner and any other liquids into mini travel bottles and secure the lids with tape – you don't want to unpack your bag to find all your clothes covered in shampoo, do you? Smaller bottles will minimise the weight of your bag, too.

- Don't forget your adapter plug for whatever country you are going to. Imagine a week without your mobile and being out of the loop on the gossip with the chicks! You can buy these at most airports. Make sure you check if it's OK to use your phone abroad if your parents pay the bill. Perhaps they could top it up to an agreed amount before you leave – and remember, texting can be cheaper than calling.

- Rolling clothes up, Swiss roll style, is better than folding them. It helps reduce wrinkles and creases.

- Don't consider going on a trip without your iPod. Listening to your fave band will help kill off any boredom, especially if your parents insist on Cliff Richard at full blast on the radio! You could rig up the mini speakers in your holiday room too, so that you can chuck on some real holiday tracks and get the vibe going.

So, Lazy Princesses, now you've packed your capsule suitcase to cover all eventualities, all you have to do now is get to the airport, sit back, relax and get super-excited about your hols!

Don't forget to drink water on the plane to keep your body in tip-top condition. All that air conditioning can wreak havoc with your skin, making you look like a dried-out old prune on arrival, and it can make your mouth so dry that you could probably use your tongue to sand down a piece of rough wood.

Always have some minty chewing gum stashed away in your handbag. Firstly, for me at least, it stops me from wanting to throw up when I'm on a long car journey, plus it helps to combat travelling bog breath.

Sarah Marley, age 11, Hardenhuish School, Wiltshire

2
Healthy Living

DID YOU KNOW that our bodies function in exactly the same way as the engine of a car? The only way a car will zoom about efficiently without breaking down is if it's topped with petrol, oil and brake fluid. Filled with mud, it would only make it to the end of the driveway (if you were lucky!).

So, if you want to work out sums and problems easily in class, have fun and not be grumpy all the time, you must feed yourself the right fuel. So steer well clear of junk food and fizzy drinks and instead fill up on lots of healthy food. Get the head chef of the family to help you on this one. Maybe your mum has got some amazing brain-fuel ideas tucked up her sleeve that all the family can munch away on.

Why Eat Well?
- Your hair, body and skin will glow so much more
- You sleep better – essential for your beauty regime
- Eating well helps combat colds, flu and other illnesses; also reduces stress levels
- You will perform better at school and in your sports
- Thumping headaches are reduced

- It cuts down the chances of you becoming obese.

And If You Don't...
- You can feel tired and sluggish
- It can make you feel stressed and irritable
- It's not so easy to fight off colds and flu
- Your hair and skin won't glow
- Eating badly can trigger off headaches, make you put weight on and feel a bit blobby
- It kills your concentration.

FOODY FACTS

- Don't go skipping meals thinking this will help you lose weight. All it does is make your metabolism slow down, which results in you putting on weight. Plus, because you're depriving your body of food, your blood-sugar levels will drop and make you feel grouchy and tired.
- If you hate to eat fruit or vegetables singly, how about blending two or three different varieties together to make a fruit smoothie?
- I know it's very glam having a chocolate croissant or a Danish pastry for breakfast (and they taste really good), but high-sugar foods on an empty stomach will give you a sugar rush for 20 minutes, followed by a mega energy crash. Try to avoid eating them and save them as an occasional treat. You're far better off going for a sugar-free muesli, a yummy bagel or porridge with chopped apple on top, all of which will keep your energy levels stable.
- If you are a sweet tooth fairy, try dried apricots for a guilt-free sugar-quenching snack.
- Sit down at the table rather than plonking yourself on the sofa to gobble down your grub. Sitting on the sofa and

eating while watching your favourite TV programme means your brain will completely forget you've been eating, resulting in you snacking on other, high-fat foods such as cheese or chocolate to keep your appetite at bay. It's also nice to sit around the table with your family, as it can quite often be the only time you get to discuss the day's events. It's surprising how days and years can go by like a flash and you have no idea what the rest of the family have been up to because you didn't make any special time to sit down and chill together.

- Revising often brings on the munchies. Exams can be stressful times and your natural instinct might be to gravitate towards the fridge every five minutes in search of comfort food, but this will only make you feel stodgy and sluggish. But if you are edging towards the fridge, make sure you are grazing on the right healthy snacks such as bananas, carrot sticks, yoghurt, dried fruit – grub that basically boosts your energy levels and metabolism.

- If you want to be a Grade-A student, avoid eating too many ready meals and takeaways – they are crammed full of hidden sugars and salts.

- It's tempting to buy fruit from market stalls at the side of the road – they tend to be cheap and it makes healthy eating easy, but rinse thoroughly. Never eat them straight away because they'll be covered in pesticides, not to mention car fumes!

- If you spend most of the year looking like Rudolf the Red-Nosed Reindeer, with one cold after another, if you suffer badly from period pains or if you're constantly tired and hungry, try zinc supplements. Zinc is renowned for zapping colds and helping those dreaded stomach cramps that you get from the time of the month. As an alternative to taking a supplement, consider introducing cheese, beef, baked beans, Brazil nuts and muesli into your diet as they are packed full of zinc. Discuss this with your mum as she or your dad will be doing the shopping. Ask them to lob some of these things into the shopping basket next time they are in the supermarket.

- Eat snacks and meals as slowly as possible. Count to ten before you scoff down anything else to give your brain time to work out whether it really wants more.

- Being thirsty can lead to poor concentration levels so think about this next time you're taking an exam. Rather than just stare at the page blankly because you're thirsty, ask if you can take some water in with you so you can sip away at your leisure.

- Coffee and tea will improve your energy and keep sleepiness at bay, but too much can leave you jittery, irritated and unable to sleep, which in turn really affects your ability to concentrate the next day. Limit yourself to just two cups of coffee or tea a day.

- Always vary your diet so you don't get bored with your food. Talk to your mum about this. Otherwise you'll be sniffing around for snacks because you don't feel satisfied.

- Carbohydrates are a short-term solution to happiness. When you feel stressed or sad, your natural tendency is to reach for something starchy and this releases the happy hormone serotonin into your brain, which makes you feel happy and chilled out. However, this can also drain your energy and make you feel tired and moody; you'll feel happy, then grumpy soon after, which makes you want to eat more and more so you feel happy again. Rye bread, brown rice, sweet potatoes, wholemeal pasta and lentils will all encourage a slow increase in blood-sugar levels, giving you more energy at a constant rate and for longer, meaning you can be the perfect little bookworm.

- Proteins such as chicken and fish give you loads of energy and, because they keep your blood-sugar levels stable, you won't go through that rollercoaster of ups and downs in your energy or mood levels often associated with teenagers.

TOP OF THE CLASS

Want to do well at school? Eating well can help you become a Grade-A student! Here's a quick run-through of recommended healthy foods to enjoy throughout the day.

Breakfast

Don't go skipping this if you're studying hard at school or for college exams – it can really affect your ability to concentrate. A good breakfast helps you concentrate during morning lessons and gives you more brainpower, especially useful for when you need to solve complicated sums in maths! Porridge, muesli or wholegrain toast are all fantastic foods as they have slow-release energy. Sugary cereals might give you a high, but then you'll have an energy slump resulting in more snacking on naughty things.

Mid-morning/Afternoon Snacks

Junk foods are the biggest concentration killers of all. I remember when I was at school, how we used to pile into the common room at about 11am to tuck into a loaf of bread and cover the slices in tons of butter, sugary jam or chocolate spread. No wonder I was half-asleep at my desk around 12pm (and I thought it was physics that put me to sleep!). So, if you want to stay awake in class and give your brain the best chance of remembering things, avoid reaching for sugary snacks such as chocolate or cereal bars, fizzy drinks, biscuits, sweets, etc. Instead opt for non-energy-draining snacks, such as bananas, dried fruits, fruit smoothies, carrot and celery sticks or nuts to keep those hunger pangs locked up and energy levels sky-high. The following is a list of foods and healthy alternatives to keep you on track. Ask your mum if she can add them to the shopping list for your household.

You want to scoff	Swap it for
Ice cream	Frozen yoghurt
Fizzy sugary drinks	Blended fruit juice with sparkling water
Crisps	Rice snacks/Pretzels
White bread	Wholemeal bread
Thick creamy savoury sauces	Tomato-based sauces
A chocolate bar	Cereal bar with nuts and raisins
Coffee	Green tea
Biscuits	Oatcakes
Chocolate	Frozen dates

Lunchtime

Every Einstein in the making knows that a stodgy lunch won't do anything for the brain, so avoid filling up on pizza, creamy pasta dishes, heavy sandwiches, crisps, sweets or fizzy drinks or you'll feel sluggish and very sleepy indeed. You won't get much revising done if you're tucked up in bed fast asleep now, will you? Rather than fuelling your body with junk that slows you down, opt for carbohydrates that offer a slow release of energy, such as brown pasta or a wholemeal-bread sarnie, a wholemeal pitta bread loaded with salad and tuna (any fish dishes, in fact, except fried fish fingers), or chicken, eggs, ham

or a hot jacket potato with salad or veg. All of these healthy options will satisfy your appetite and fill your tummy, plus your brainpower will be boosted, you'll have loads of energy and your time at school will whiz by.

- Dinner/bedtime drinks to help you sleep well – camomile tea or hot milk.

FOOD POWER

There is such a thing as magic food – food that can do amazing things to your mind and body just by you simply gobbling it down. Some have the power to increase your concentration and make your skin glow like gold and some can make your skin look as dull as dirty dish water (ie processed food and sugary sweets). So learn this next little section off by heart, princesses, so that you too can gleam like a sparkling jewel. And next time you see your parents heading off to the supermarket, put this list right under their noses so that your cupboards are constantly filled with a supply of beauty and brainpower fodder!

Simon Cowell – Pop Impresario

I wasn't particularly academic at school and I didn't realise the value of a good breakfast. Now, every morning, I have a bowl of porridge which slowly releases energy during my busy day. You can also add raisins and banana for a bit of extra fibre if you wish.

Foods That Boost Your Concentration
- Water (about eight glasses a day is recommended – distilled or bottled if it's in the house)
- Porridge oats
- Sugar-free muesli
- Dark chocolate. Dark chocolate on average has fewer calories, more fibre, fewer carbs and less cholesterol than white or milk chocolate. It's also a lot more natural than the others. Studies have shown that dark chocolate has eight times more antioxidants (the stuff that keeps us looking younger and helps our body rid itself of harmful toxins) than strawberries! So if you are a choccie lover, then isn't this the best news ever? Only a few squares mind! Don't overdo it!
- Salmon
- Mackerel
- Anchovies
- Flax seeds
- Eggs
- Milk
- Avocados
- Popcorn – plain
- Wholegrains
- Wholewheat
- Camomile tea
- Blueberries

Foods to Get Rid of Stomach Gas
- Fennel tea
- Fresh sage
- Kiwi fruits
- Leeks
- Melon

Foods to De-Bloat Your Tummy

- Asparagus
- Lettuce
- Kiwi fruits
- Melon
- Leeks

Foods to Stave Off Hunger

- Tuna
- Tofu
- Courgettes
- Mushrooms
- Avocados
- Water
- Bulgur wheat

Foods to Make Your Skin and Hair Glow

- Apples
- Water (about eight glasses a day)
- Strawberries
- Blackberries
- Mackerel
- Mangoes
- Broccoli
- Kale
- Fennel
- Sweet potatoes

Foods That Help Your Digestion

- Peppermint tea
- Honey
- Figs

- Papaya
- Fresh mint

Foods to Rehydrate You
- Watermelon
- Melon
- Cucumbers
- Tomatoes
- Lettuce

What to Eat and Drink to Sleep Better
- Camomile tea
- Bananas

Foods to Calm Painful PMS and Reduce Mood Swings
- Brown rice
- Peaches
- Oats
- Apricots
- Lentils
- Edamame beans

Foods to Reduce Munchie Attacks and Cravings
- Brown rice
- Tuna
- Barley
- Grapes
- Melon
- Rye
- Oats
- Peaches
- Grapefruit

- Pears
- Sweet potatoes

Foods to Get Rid of Trapped Poos

- Soya beans
- Figs
- Apricots
- Seeds – sunflower, pumpkin and sesame are all good
- Water (about eight glasses a day)
- Courgettes
- Liquorice
- Broccoli
- Fennel and mint teas
- Green, red or white cabbage
- Olives
- Bananas
- Oats
- Pears
- Chicory
- Peaches
- Honey
- Prunes
- Spinach
- Grapes
- Cucumber

Food and Drink to Calm You

- Ricotta cheese
- Bio yoghurt
- Green tea
- Grapes
- Spinach

- Blueberries
- Oats
- Almonds
- Garlic
- Asparagus
- Avocados
- Red peppers
- Celery
- Camomile tea

Foods to Protect You From Colds and Other Infections
- Prawns
- Turkey
- Citrus fruits, such as limes, oranges and lemons
- Chillies
- Watercress
- Chickpeas
- Mangoes
- Tomatoes
- Red peppers
- Duck
- Cherries
- Spinach
- Ginger
- Bio yoghurt

Foods for Strong Bones
- Mackerel
- Blueberries
- Milk
- Kale
- Oats

Foods to Boost Your Energy

- Lentils
- Grapefruit
- Sunflower seeds
- Eggs – try not to eat them every day as they can make you constipated. Have them about three times a week.
- Bananas
- Brown rice
- Bulgur wheat
- Rye
- Mushrooms
- Chicory
- Water (about eight glasses a day)
- Oats
- Sweet potatoes
- Spinach
- Chickpeas

Foods to Get Rid of Bad Breath

- Beetroot

Alesha Dixon – Singer

Try avocado on toast. Why? Because it tastes great!

ıt

. ... sley (especially good for garlic breath)

So there you have it, lovely ladies – a crash course on how you can munch your way to the top of the class and how to trough it (healthily of course) until you are a hot honey.

PERIODS AND HOW TO HANDLE THEM

What is it about periods that makes us so snappy and down in the dumps? It's a bit like an alien taking over our body for a week, isn't it? It makes us eat like an industrial vacuum cleaner, consuming everything that crosses our path. It makes us wake up in a fluster, go to bed in an even bigger fluster, we have a constant tummy ache and it makes us do ridiculous things like walk out of the house with shoes that don't even match! So, here are a few little ways to make you feel less like a blob and more of a blooming beauty!

- PMT can sometimes put you in a terrible mood, but don't let it ruin your day. Instead, fight back. When you get up, tell yourself you're going to have a great day and that you're the coolest chick alive. Even if it's a weekday and you have to wear your school uniform, look as smart and groomed as you can. Walk out of the house as if you're the most beautiful girl on the planet (you are!). Positive thinking works wonders.
- If you want to release some imprisoned anger, go home, walk into your bedroom, close the door and scream as loudly as possible into a pillow. Trust me, it works! Far better than shouting at your mum or best friend, too.
- So that you leave the house feeling confident and comfortable and not like you're transporting a small mattress around with you, try a brand of sanitary towel

such as Always Ultra. They are brilliant as they stick to your pants like padlocks, they are super-absorbent and help to keep flow away from the edges, meaning you can feel secure and happy for the duration of your period.

- Don't forget to take a little stash of sanitary protection around with you at all times (Tampax Compak are brilliant as they are tiny and super-easy to use). Disguise them in a cute little fabric container or bag in case your bag falls open. You know how cruel boys can be!

- If, for some reason, you have an accident and leak through to your clothes, fear not. Wrap your cardigan or jumper around your waist and cruise off to the loos.

- If someone comes up to tell you that you have leaked on the back of your outfit, style it out like a cool cucumber. All you have to do is act the opposite to how you are actually feeling. Pretend that you are OK with it and go off and sort it out immediately. At no point show how embarrassed you feel. The less embarrassment you show, the quicker the whole scenario will die down.

- Never use hot water to remove blood stains from your clothing as this will set the blood and you will never be able to remove it. When you see a stain, act immediately – if you can remove the garment then take it off and rinse it under cold running water. If this isn't possible because you are out and about, quickly dash off to the bathroom, grab a big bunch of loo roll or those big paper hand towels, dunk them under the cold water and gently dab the stained area. Whatever you do, don't scrub or rub too hard. This will only encourage it to spread even more into the fibres of your clothing. Keep replacing the loo roll for a fresh wet piece. If you sort a blood stain out immediately, then you won't be left with a permanent mark.

- Self-conscious on period days? Wear dark-coloured clothes. Definitely give white clothes a miss if you don't feel comfortable.
- If your tummy really aches, try going out for a brisk walk or a little jog. Exercise will make you feel better and lift your mood.
- You can also hug up to a hot water bottle or take a warm bath to relieve cramps and lower back pain. Aromatherapy oils are a real treat and will relax you.
- If you know that you're not feeling yourself and you think you might snap at someone for no reason, let them know you have your period so they won't take your grumpiness personally.
- At the end of a busy day, try to relax. Sit back and listen to calming music. The more relaxed you are, the better your period pains. If you're stressed, they will kick in with a vengeance.
- If your lower back or tummy is really hurting, pop a hot water bottle on them to relieve the pain.
- Our bodies change so much when we start our periods and it's completely normal to put on a bit of weight and grow a bit taller. Just exercise regularly and try to stick to a healthy, nutritious diet.
- Always wear cotton knickers during your period so that your 'front flower' can breathe.
- If you will be hitting the pool or the seawater, always wear a tampon. Be sure the string is nicely tucked into your swimming costume and not dangling out, though! Keep your swim as short as possible and avoid being in your swimming costume for too long as your tampon time might just run out.
- To avoid being caught out by surprise by your period, keep track by marking the beginning and the end of each one in

your diary so you know exactly when to expect it. Give your mum the heads up when you have your period so that she can keep the bathroom cupboard stocked with an emergency supply at all times.

- Periods can zap the iron from our bodies, making us feel super-tired. Iron supplements can help, so ask your mum to visit the chemist with you to find out what's available and suitable for your age.

- Never wear a tampon any longer than six hours. Any longer and you risk Toxic Shock Syndrome (TSS). TSS is a rare bacterial illness often associated with women who use super-absorbent tampons. Some of the symptoms are a rash, headaches, vomiting, sudden high fever or diarrhoea. To avoid getting this potentially life-threatening illness, change your tampon regularly – at least every 4–6 hours and maybe use the lowest-absorbency tampons possible. So don't go leaving one wedged in there all day long, OK, girlies?

Sinitta

That time of the month that women often despise, I think, should be turned into a pamper week. Your body is cleansing and rejuvenating, so why not use that time to cleanse and rejuvenate your hair, skin, nails and toes! Take each day to focus on another part of your body so that, by the end of the week, you are a glowing goddess. A few pounds lighter, refreshed, rested and lovely!

- It makes sense not to wear your best undies when you're having your period. Instead, wear older ones in a dark colour.
- A lovely cup of camomile tea will help to relax cramping and makes you sleep better too.
- Have a good old chinwag with your mum about all of the ins and outs about the dreaded time of the month. If anyone knows it inside out, it's her! So, if you have any questions, ask her to explain and tell her what you are going through.
- Another bummer of getting your period is greasy hair, plus you might look a bit on the pale side. So, you know what I do? I pop on bright clothes that inject colour into my complexion and that automatically make me feel happy and I wear some blusher to put some colour back into my ghost-like face.

SLEEP LIKE A BABY

Do you sometimes find yourself in LaLa land, happily dreaming away about Zac Efron proposing to you on a deserted white beach, while being showered on a daily basis with thousands of pounds' worth of clothes and diamonds from all of the big fashion houses, because you happen to be the coolest pop star in the universe?

OK, so using your desk as your makeshift pillow and falling asleep right under your teacher's nose might not be the brightest idea in the textbook, but does this happen often and if so, why? Getting the right amount of sleep works wonders and can really affect your personality and mood, not to mention your looks. Lack of sleep can turn a perfectly sweet, gorgeous and well-mannered girl into a gremlin. Follow these tips to get a good night's sleep, every time.

- Eating a big meal late at night, hoovering up sugary food or feeling stressed about something are all major culprits behind missed zzzzzs. Try to eat less in the evening, avoid sugary junk foods and try to relax for at least an hour before you hit the sack in a lovely bath.

- If you're feeling peckish before you go to bed, don't stuff yourself with chocolate biscuits or penny sweets – they are full of naughty sugars, which will only keep you awake and annoyed, so eat a banana instead because they are very calming indeed.

- Make sure the heating in your room isn't on full blast. The cooler and more aerated your environment, the better you will sleep.

- Relax before you go to bed. A deluxe bath may be just the ticket you may need, especially if you've had a stressful day at school. Fill your bath with bubble bath, roll a towel up and plonk it on the end of the bath top to use as a headrest, and turn on some relaxing music. Think of somewhere in the world that you have visited and loved. It could be a stunning beach holiday or an amazing walk in a flower-filled meadow. Fill your mind with lots of positive thoughts like this to get rid of stressful negative ones.

- Try drinking a lovely warm mug of milk before you go to bed – this will lull you into a nice cosy sleep.

- Don't do your homework too late in the evening – this will keep your brain ticking, therefore making it very hard for you to relax.

- To switch off at night, I always read one of my favourite magazines.

- Make sure your room is dark. Sunlight streaming through will wake you up in no time! If there's an annoying gap in the curtain that always wakes you up, sleep with a black-out mask on, or ask your dad to put up a black-out blind for you to go behind your already existing curtains in the recess.

- I always find chilled-out music (no words, just instruments) lulls me into a sleepy state of mind and, before I know it, I'm off in fairyland.

- When your alarm rings in the morning, get up straight away and don't hit the snooze button. Snoozing actually makes you feel more tired and a little bit grumpy, plus your body goes into shutdown mode. Get up and get going!

- Is your mattress comfortable? If not, ask your parents if you can have a new one, but test them out in the shop first to find one that suits you. You should turn mattresses regularly so they stay firm and so that they don't mould into the shape of your body. If you keep turning them over and around, they will stay even all over, which will stop you from getting a sore back.

- After your mattress, your pillow is the next most important item for a good night's sleep. I take mine everywhere! Quite possibly, it's the best-travelled pillow in the universe. A good pillow will make you sleep like a baby, so make sure no one else in the house nicks it.

- Doing exercise at least three times a week is great for a constant sleep pattern. Go for a 30-minute run round the block or a good brisk walk with your chums. Mind you, don't do it just before you go to bed or you'll zing with energy and be unable to sleep.

- Avoid drinking caffeine at night. If you like a hot drink before you go to bed, substitute coffee or tea for camomile tea or a hot chocolate.

- Don't just lie there, worrying or thinking – all you'll do is get yourself in a stew. Instead, get up and do something to take your mind off the fact that you can't sleep. When you feel a bit dozy, you can get back into bed and nod off. Talk to your parents if you're worried. Go down and see them for a while – they might well be able to help.

- If your clock has an annoying tick-tock, get a new one that doesn't make any noise at all. Otherwise, you'll end up counting every single tick-tock, if you're anything like me!

- Earplugs are perfect if you live in a noisy family or on a main road. Plug 'em in to block out the noise.

- If you wake up looking exhausted due to a lack of sleep, pop a whole tray of ice cubes into a mixing bowl, add a pint or so of cold water and leave for five minutes until the water is really, really cold. Dip a flannel or T-towel in the ice-cold water, squeeze it out and lie down, either on the floor or on your bed. Hold the cloth over your eyes for about five to seven minutes. When the flannel becomes warm, just dip it back in the cold water and start again. This will help reduce any puffiness around your eyes, plus it will soothe them.

- An untidy room means an untidy mind! Only ever hop into bed once your room is neat and tidy. Waking up to a messy room just makes you feel cluttered and irritated in the morning.

- Eating healthy foods and cutting down on junk food gives you stacks more energy and also helps you sleep well at night, so make sure you get your five portions of fruit and veg a day and drink plenty of water (about eight glasses a day).

BOOST YOUR ENERGY LEVELS

Do you sometimes feel like you're dragging two concrete blocks around with you on the end of your legs and your eyes are so tired that you need a couple of matches to keep them open? And it's only 2pm! Well, princesses, with a few little lotions and potions, plus a wave of the magic wand you'll soon be getting a good night's sleep – lots of shut-eye makes you feel more alert and there are other things you can do, too. Just follow my tips.

- With the right food, you will perform better at school and also sleep well (see pages 81–90 for advice on this).
- Baths and calming instrumental music will help you wind down at the end of a busy day.
- At the end of your shower in the morning, quickly blast yourself in cold water to blow away any cobwebs.
- Rub and massage your scalp vigorously when you're washing your hair in the shower to revitalise.
- When you are washing your face, a lovely three- or four-minute massage will get the blood pumping and can be quite invigorating. Finish off by splashing with cold water.
- If you're exhausted, your eyes will let everyone know. Try lying back with a couple of ice-cold wet teabags on your eyes for ten minutes to revive them.
- Have a bath and put lots of lovely fresh herbs, such as mint and rosemary, in it. These herbs are known for their invigorating properties.
- Sometimes, being bored with life can trigger tiredness. If this is the case, set yourself a target each day. Do something you wouldn't normally do and get out of your comfort zone. For instance, this could be something that you have always felt nervous about. How about running in a fun run and raising some dosh for your favourite charity, or even entering a competition of some sort? Do it, and sooner or later it will become the norm and your confidence will increase. What a great satisfying feeling, eh?
- Seeing as your feet have to carry you around all day long, why

not treat them to something you know they will love? Fill a bowl with hot water and throw in a handful of sea salt and some mint or flower petals. Now take it into the living room, pop your fave TV programme on, sit on the sofa and dip your tootsies in. Leave to soak for 15 minutes. Pat dry afterwards with a towel, then moisturise with a mint foot cream.

- Fresh air is a great way to perk up your energy levels, especially if you are indoors a lot of the time studying. Take in big long breaths of air so lots of oxygen enters your system while you're out and about.

- Stand in front of a mirror and sing a line from a really upbeat song, not forgetting the moves, of course! Now say to yourself out loud that you are fabulous. This will make you feel happy with a little buzzy edge.

DON'T WORRY, BE HAPPY!

Are you one of those girls who is constantly forgetting things, or maybe you're always in a fluster and getting your knickers in a twist? If so, you need to stop for a few minutes, get yourself organised and start again. Here's how.

- Before you go to bed, make a list of what you need to do the next morning. Put the clothes that you want to wear out on a chair and put away anything you don't need. Check your timetable and fill your school bag with the books you need, pack sports and other equipment. This will save you stacks of time in the morning and prevent you from rocking up late for school or work – and a lot less stressed.

- If something is genuinely worrying you, there's no better way of resolving it than to discuss your feelings with someone in your family. A problem shared is a problem solved.

- During studying time, always have a big bunch of flowers or foliage by your desk. When you feel tense, sniff them. The more oxygen you inhale (that's what they give off), the calmer you'll feel.

- Keep a pot of honey in the kitchen cupboard and, when you feel as if your brains about to explode, dip your finger in it and suck the honey off. Honey makes you feel less stressed and happy again because it releases a happy hormone called serotonin.

- Don't play your hectic banging music – this will make your mood go from bad to worse. Instead, try playing and even singing along to Christmas songs. 'Silent Night' is a good 'un! Or how about some spiritual chilled-out music to de-stress? Download tracks without lyrics so you can dreamily drift away and forget your troubles for a moment.

- Do you sometimes notice how dogs find a really weird place to snooze, whether it's on top of the back of the sofa, or with their heads hidden behind the bookcase, and how relaxed they always look? Well, take a leaf out of their book! Find a place in your home where you feel really, really relaxed. I love to lie under the kitchen table with a pillow and always have done so since I was a little girl. Often I find my sister in the airing cupboard because it's so warm and cosy! So, wherever this place might be, visit it when you feel stress is really getting you down and sit or lie there for ten minutes and let your thoughts just drift away.

- I've got a great little stress buster and that's stroking your pet. It's scientifically proven to work. I mean, I can't think how many times my poor doggies have had to sit there and listen to my worries and, although they can't answer back, they always seem to help. I also think it has something to do with the fact that the constant stroking rhythm lulls us into a chilled-out mode and, whatever secret we tell them, we know they aren't going to blab it.

- If you've been studying in your room all day, open up the windows for a few minutes every few hours. That whoosh of oxygen will do wonders for your foggy head and will get rid of any stuffiness.

- Turn on MTV and pretend you're one of Justin Timberlake's backing dancers. Make all of your moves hot and totally exaggerated. This really will pop the stress bubble! Just make sure you've closed the curtains beforehand. You don't want that boy you fancy to suddenly walk past the house and see you in full swing!

- Have a day where you abandon the TV, your mobile and your computer. Sometimes it's good to give yourself a break and allow yourself to feel free.

- Studying for exams can be extremely stressful. Every hour, give yourself a break and do something completely different to take your mind off things, if only for about ten minutes. This will really refresh your memory and brainpower so you're ready for another stint of studying. Try a ten-minute brisk walk around the block, give yourself a home facial or brew yourself a cuppa.

- Phone your best friend for a giggle and gossip.

MORE MOOD BOOSTERS

- Now, this might sound a bit bonkers, but it really does work. If you get a bit stressed and anxious, especially around the dreaded exam time, then it's time to schedule in a little Hannah remedy that's natural and fun – yep, a wee countryside excursion. It's essential that you take your camera – you'll be taking pictures of sheep, bark and running water, etc. Believe it or not, those elements of nature will really relax you.

- Develop your favourite pictures into big sizes (blow them up on a photocopying machine), those that make you feel happy and soothed (a sheep in a green field works wonders for me), and then hang them up on the wall near your bed. When you feel a bit down, lie back on your bed and stare at your pictures, daydream away and remember those special moments. You could, of course, also do this with holiday pictures that mean a lot to you and put you in a chirpy mood.

- If you are terrible at arriving at places on time, put your clock forward by ten minutes so that hopefully you will arrive bang on time and feel less flustered.

- Colourful clothes always put me in a good mood.

- If you get headaches regularly, avoid asking your mum for pills every time. Instead, try massaging lavender oil on your temples or place a cold, wet flannel (straight from the fridge) on your forehead to soothe the pain. Also, try drinking more water (up to eight glasses a day is recommended) – you may just be dehydrated, especially if you spend a lot of time in front of a computer. Of course, if your headache persists, consult your GP.

- If you are already stressed, try to cut down on anything with caffeine in it, such as coca-cola, tea and coffee. They just make your stress levels worse. Instead, opt for a relaxing herbal tea.

- Sweets may give you a short burst of energy, but too much of anything sugary means a high, followed by a slump.

- Finally, steer clear of white bread and fried foods too as these will drain you of energy and make you feel even more stressed due to their having little nutritional value.

FACTS ABOUT WATER

- 70% of our body is made up of water.
- Drinking water (eight glasses per day) cleanses and hydrates our skin; it also prevents our eyes feeling dry and keeps bowel movements regular.
- Water fills you up and stops you from feeling peckish. Sometimes your body mistakes thirst for hunger. Before you allow your monster munch hand to delve in the biscuit barrel, drink a glass of water to see if your craving for food disappears.
- Finally, it boosts your energy levels and stops you feeling groggy and tired.

FIGHT THOSE FARTS!

Why are farts so hilarious? Why is it, when somebody farts, we all roll around on the floor in absolute fits of hysterics, pinching our noses, pulling faces and trying not to pee ourselves? Our bums have a mind of their own and, when those cheeky bottoms want to burp, there's absolutely nothing you can do about it. You do everything in your power to keep the toxic fumes locked up (especially if you are on a hot date in the cinema), you squeeze in your bum cheeks, go red in the face, count to 10 and pray it just disappears. But it doesn't, does it?

- If you let one rip, blame it on a dog poo that must have got stuck to somebody's shoe. Tell everyone to lift up their feet to check and then pretend you have it on your shoe and go outside to get rid of it on the grass. If there's a dog around, blame it on him!
- Light a match and blow it out after four seconds. This is a beauty for disguising any rancid smells that have forced themselves out from your bottom.

- Sprinkle thyme or mint on your food to help prevent excess wind. It's also really important to drink plenty of fluids such as water and herbal teas (not fizzy drinks).
- The smell of freshly peeled oranges will freshen up any room a treat, so always carry one in your bag. If you accidentally let rip, peel your orange and no one will know.
- Don't guzzle your food back without chewing or your stomach will look like a hot-air balloon! Chomp, chomp, chomp food thoroughly to reduce wind.
- Trapped farts can sometimes be really painful and will ruin the look of a fitted dress. If this happens to you, sneak off to the nearest bathroom, and lock the door (believe me, you really don't want anyone seeing what you're about to do!). Get on your hands and knees (sort of like a yoga position). Now arch your bum as high in the air as possible to create a triangle shape (your bum being the very highest point). Hold for three or four minutes. This forces the wind right up to your bum. Now, lower your bum back down towards the floor and with any luck this should release the trapped stinker. When you wander back into the room, your tummy will look surfboard flat again.
- We all love a little fizzy lemonade or cola, but for some chicks this can ruin the look of a tight frock as these drinks can fill your stomach up with lots of unwanted wind that causes gut ache. Instead, opt for non-fizzy drinks.
- If you're going out for a big dinner and you know you get really bad wind, take a handful of chopped fresh coriander in a plastic bag in your handbag. Sneakily sprinkle it over your food. Coriander is a great tonic for your body in many ways. It helps to prevent farts from brewing up, it helps to relieve trapped wind and it's great for digestion. So, all in all, it's great for sorting wind and storm damage out.

- If you really can't hold it in, wait for something loud to happen: a car, bus or fire engine driving past, even a blast of music will all provide the right moment!

WEE WATCH

- After you've had a wee, have a peek down the loo. If it's super-stinky and a dark-yellow or orange colour and makes your nostril hairs curl up, then you are dehydrated. Your pee should be the colour of a pale yellow diamond, so glug down lots of water and herbal teas.
- If your pee is really cloudy, you may be eating too much sugary foods or dairy. Try adding some sweet potatoes or aduki beans to your diet.
- Running to the loo every five minutes? It's possible you may be drinking too many soft or caffeine-filled drinks that are crammed with bad sugars. Try eating kidney beans, salmon and parsley to combat this.
- However, if you're concerned about your wee, then talk to your mum and perhaps seek medical advice.

BEAT THE ITCH!

For some people, hay fever can make the spring and summer months a real nightmare. As soon as pretty flowers start to bloom and bees get hard to work pollinating them, so too do the sneezing, itching and headaches begin. Here's how to keep the dreaded pollen at bay.

- Wear a big pair of sunnies (I mean, Mary-Kate Olsen style) to keep the pollen that causes irritation away from your eyes.
- If you've been out and about near plants and flowers, wash your hair and change your clothes. This will help reduce the amount of pollen around you, plus it's especially important

if you are going to bed – you don't want pollen rubbing off on to your pillow.

- During the hay fever season, don't hang clothes out to dry because pollen will stick to the wet garments, especially when it's windy. This will then fire up the symptoms of hay fever when you pop them on once they're dry. Instead, hang clothing on an indoor line or use the tumble dryer. Ask your mum if she can damp dust (that means dusting with a damp cloth). This prevents dust from going up in the air and straight into your face. If the cloth is damp, then the dust will stick to it.

- Bathe your scratchy eyes in cold water three times a day to soothe them.

- Smear some Vaseline inside each nostril. This will help to capture any pollen before it goes up your nose.

- If you wear contact lenses and you are off to a barbecue or maybe you're helping out in the garden, avoid putting them in – grass pollen will get in your eyes and become trapped under the lenses, resulting in very itchy eyes indeed.

- If your dad asks you to help trim the lawn, tell him sorry but it's off the menu and he'll have to do it himself! Exposure to cut grass and leaves, etc. can trigger itchy eyes, sneezing and headaches. If there's no way of getting out of it, pop on some goggles, wrap your face in a scarf, put a shower cap on and go tackle the job!

- When you are cruising along in a car during the hay fever season, try to keep the windows closed so the pollen doesn't sneak in.

- Keep dogs and cats super-clean, especially if they like rolling around in the grass. Pollen may become wedged in their fur, which can then be transferred to you when you squeeze a little hug out of them.

FIT AND FABULOUS!

Of course, every girl would like never-ending peachy pins, a washboard stomach and a bottom that looks like two perfect buns, but, let's be honest, this won't happen if you spend half of your life parked up on the sofa, ramming cupcakes and burgers down your throat while working your way through every single film from the local video shop! It's exercise that you need.

Keeping fit doesn't necessarily mean padlocking yourself to the running machine at the gym until you go red in the face and pass out, or cycling nowhere on one of those stationary bikes. If you don't like the gym, don't go! It's as simple as that, but you do need to find another way of doing exercise, and here's how!

- Turn the house into a gym palace. Run up and down the stairs holding a bag of sugar in each hand as weights (you can use anything, really) until your legs and bum cheeks are quivering. Do this at least 30 times.
- Do your errands in your trainers; run from one place to another. Not only will you get everything done in a super-quick time, but you'll also burn lots of calories, tone up and it won't cost you a penny.
- If you're popping out to do some shopping or meet your friends, rather than being lazy and hopping on the bus, try going by foot instead.
- The more fun the exercise is, the more likely you'll do it. Perfect examples are gardening or helping a friend rearrange her bedroom. Get right in there and offer your services.
- If you find it hard to exercise, at weekends, put your gym kit on as soon as you've showered and see if this encourages you to get moving.

- Exercising in the evening means you'll end up feeling full of beans and unable to sleep. If you go in the morning, you will kickstart your metabolism and burn calories for the rest of the day – you'll also feel full of energy, too.

- Next time you need to get a fresh box of teabags or hot chocolate from the top of the shelf, don't take the easy option and get a chair to clamber on to. Instead, lean up on tiptoes and reach and stretch for Britain! This is a great way to stretch out your back and spine – perfect when you've been sitting down studying all day long.

- Whenever you are standing waiting (for the kettle to boil, for instance, or if you're on the phone), don't just stand there doing nothing. Squeeze your bum cheeks as hard as possible, hold for ten seconds and then release. Repeat ten times.

- You can also take this opportunity to do some exercises such as calf raises while holding on to the edge of the worktop. Or do some bicep curls while holding two bags of sugar or two cans of baked beans – a great way of toning up those arm muscles!

- If you're chained to your desk due to studying and have no hope of getting in a bit of exercise, don't worry. Try doing some sneaky stomach exercises while you work. All you have to do is breathe in and, when you exhale, tense your stomach muscles, hold for ten seconds and then release. Do this about 15 times and I promise you will start to get a surfboard-like tummy!

- Make your bed every morning and burn 20 calories! This one is a seriously good way of clocking up some much-needed brownie points with your mum, too.

- If your mum already has a workout video stashed away in the back of the TV cupboard, ask if you can borrow it. If not, don't go out and buy one specially – it's a waste of money. Instead, put MTV on full blast, dance for 20 minutes and work up a good old sweat. Great exercise, and it's fun too! Ask your mum and sister, you never know, they might just like to join in! Another idea if you want some good music to do your dance routines to, but don't really want to spend that much money, is to hot-foot it down to your library and borrow a fitness DVD from there, or try your local car boot sale – they always have bundles of music for hardly anything.

- See if your mum will buy a cordless phone so that every time you make a call to your best chum for a ten-hour marathon chat, you can walk around the place getting fit, rather than sitting on your bum cheeks, tied to the wall.

- Ditch the remote control! When you want to change TV channels, get up and switch them manually. You'll burn more calories getting up and down than moving just one finger.

- Always take the stairs. Try not to use the escalator or lift unless it's an emergency.

- If you have to take the escalator, walk up it rather than waiting for it to transport you to the top.

- Nothing beats a good old chinwag with your best gal pal in the local coffee shop, but, instead of sitting there, ask for a takeaway and walk, gossip and drink your tea around the park. This is another great way of squeezing in some light exercise while having something yummy to drink.

- There are two reasons why you should eat with chopsticks. First, it takes you four times longer to eat your dinner, so it's much more satisfying because you take many more mouthfuls so you feel you're eating more. Normally it would take all of three seconds with a knife and fork. Second, because chopsticks are really difficult to use, they force you to focus on your meal, therefore you concentrate on what you're eating, not what's on TV. Again, it's a satisfying feeling for the brain as it remembers that you've eaten and you'll be less likely to reach for the naughty snacks later.

- When you go to a party, don't be the loser wedged on the corner of the sofa. Get up and dance your little cotton socks off! Having a rock and roll time, cutting some mean dance shapes is one of the best ways to get fit.

- If you want to stop snacking on something, then brush your teeth. The minty fresh taste will put you off!

- Everybody needs encouragement when it comes to doing exercise. If you wear cool, trendy, workout gear that makes you feel good, you'll be down the gym in no time at all. But if your kit looks like an ancient car-seat cover, you won't want to put it on at all, so you'll never work up a sweat. Get yourself some cool gym kit now! It doesn't have to be pricey.

- I just LOVE hula-hoops! All that twisting and twirling does wonders for toning up your tummy.

- Skipping too is an excellent way to get fit. Just make sure you don't do it in your living room while watching TV. Smashing all the vases and lampshades, etc. may just permit your parents to ground you for the next 30 years!

- I always look like I've got ants in my pants – I never really sit still. I'm always twiddling and fidgeting – even at night when I'm in my bed, I'm like a Jack-in-the-box! Although at times I probably look a little on the mad side, I'm actually doing my body a lot of good. The more you fidget, the more you tense your muscles! The more muscle you build, the more calories you burn! It's just a bonus in the 'light' exercise area.

- Here's the laziest ever way of doing stomach crunches –

when you're next sitting down, watching an episode of *Hannah Montana*, hold your tummy muscles in really tight for a minute, then relax. Repeat five times. The great thing about this exercise is that you can do it absolutely anywhere.

- Next time you're brushing your teeth, stand on one leg and lift your other leg up to the side and back down. Repeat about ten times and then do the other leg!

- You know when someone's sitting down and they want to fart then they kind of lean over to one side and lift one bum cheek, don't they? Well, this next exercise is similar, but the difference is, you'll be doing undercover bum-cheek clenches instead. All you have to do is squeeze your bum for one minute, then relax and repeat another five times. If you do this every day, you'll soon have a bum that looks and feels as firm as a peach.

So you see, being a lean bean and keeping fit and fabulous isn't that hard after all!

Amie-Jane Hadley, Age 13, The Kingswinford School, West Midlands

3
Sparkle Like a Princess

WHEN THEY LOOK at the fridge, a lot of girls think pork-out sessions, munchie attacks and snacks. I know I did, back in the days when I used to do a very good impression of a Henry Hoover – you know, one of those super-sucking greedy machines that don't leave a crumb in sight (your mum probably has one stashed away under the stairs at home). But your fridge can also be a valuable source of beauty treatments. Yep, all those lip-smacking treats are actually your ticket to looking one step closer to your fave celebrity. It's as easy as that! Get ready to blast and blend your way to beautiful skin.

LOVE THE SKIN YOU'RE IN

Before you create any homemade facial preparations, make sure the kitchen utensils that you use are completely clean. Check to see if your mum is cool with this first. Wooden spoons tend to absorb all kinds of flavours and smells, so you're better off going for a metal or plastic one. If you want to use a wooden spoon, ask your mum to buy you a cheapie from the local supermarket that you can use specifically for beautifying and store it somewhere safely away from the one used for spag bol! Remember, sharing is caring – so ask your mum if she wants to either join in making the goodies or at least try them once they have been made! It doesn't matter how old you are, all us chicks (including grannies) love a bit of beautifying.

The other good thing about making your own princess pampering products is that they are not only cheaper, but you also know exactly what has gone into making them. One thing to bear in mind, though, is that these homemade beauty products don't really have a long shelf life and all need to be used straight away.

For starters, treat your face to a deep-cleansing mask. It will draw out all the grub from your pores, dislodge the congestion that causes spots and pep your skin back to perkiness by smoothing and brightening it.

Lemon & Tea Mask

1 teaspoon brewed tea (make it strong!)
1 teaspoon fresh lemon juice
1½ tablespoons milk powder
1 teaspoon egg white, whisked or beaten into froth

Simply mix the tea and lemon juice together, then sprinkle in the milk powder and egg white. Splodge the gooey mixture over your face, leave for 20 minutes and sit back and listen to some chilled music, then rinse off with warm water and moisturise.

- It's always better to wash your face with warm water (which will allow the pores to open up and be cleaned inside) and then rinse with cold water so that the pores close back up again, which will stop dirt from working its way back in again.

- You should exfoliate your skin twice a week. This will prevent the pores from clogging up, which usually results in spots, especially if you wear a lot of base make-up. Exfoliating removes all the dead skin cells allowing your skin to breathe more easily.

- For a brilliant DIY facial scrub at home, mix two tablespoons each of sugar and lemon juice together and massage GENTLY over your skin for a minute or two. Exfoliate away till you look like a gleaming princess!

- Mash up a banana with a little milk and spoon it on to your fabulous face for a great natural moisturiser if you have run out of the real stuff.

- If you are feeling a bit under the weather, this can really reflect in your skin, so take your face into the kitchen and steam cuisine it! Yep, a hot steamy session will leave your complexion cleansed and lush again. Note: this treatment is not suitable for sensitive skins, however. Fill a bowl with hot water, lean your cleansed face over it and then cover your head in a tea towel. After ten minutes of steaming, uncover yourself, splash your face with lukewarm running water to close up the pores and gently pat dry with a clean towel.

- Give your face a two-minute massage every day using your face cream. Gently massage upwards and outwards; do not drag your skin. This is a great ritual that you should continue until you become an old granny! It's brilliant for keeping those ageing lines under control.

- Now, I know how boring drinking water can be, almost a chore at times, hey, but it really is one of the cheapest and most effective ways of making your skin sparkle like a diamond because it flushes out toxins from your system. The recommended daily amount is 1.5 litres (or about eight glasses) a day, but if you feel like you're forcing it down, how about herbal tea? There are so many yummy flavours available at the supermarket. Do your best to lay off the sugary fizzy drinks, too, as they are really not that good for your teeth. Ask your mum if she can work one mackerel fillet per week into your diet (serve with a salad) – it will give your complexion a clear and healthy glow.

- Did you know that often hunger is due to dehydration? Always drink some water before you eat. I carry a little bottle of water in my bag with me at all times so that I can sip as and when I like.

- My next tip is best done in the kitchen where you can make lots of mess, but make sure you clear up afterwards! For oily (not sensitive) skin, blend two ripe tomatoes with two tablespoons natural live yoghurt (or ask one of your parents to do this for you). Massage into a cleansed face and leave for about 15 minutes. Rinse off with warm water and moisturise.

- Here's another quick DIY fresh-food facial for when you're in the shower. Get a small cup of brown sugar, jump in the shower, rub a bar of wet soap in your hands, dip them in the sugar and gently scrub your body and face to remove dead skin cells. Rub very carefully over your face though as it's a lot more sensitive than your body. You can repeat this process once every 7–10 days.

- Blend a big slice of watermelon in a kitchen blender (or get one of your parents to do this with you) and apply directly to a cleansed face. It's an excellent natural cleanser and you can eat the leftovers!

- Blast a small cup of porridge oats in a kitchen blender with enough warm water to form a thick creamy consistency. Massage into your face to exfoliate your skin. You can do this once every 7–10 days.

- For more beauty treatments and to find out how to treat your friends to a relaxing spa session, see pages 188–97.

SLEEPING BEAUTY

Late nights, lack of sleep and not enough water is the perfect recipe for dried-out, prune-like skin. In fact, faces robbed of moisture and a good meal (lotions and potions) are usually accessorised with dark carrier bags under the eyes, a sprinkling of unsightly spots and a grey concrete texture. This is where the phrase 'beauty sleep' comes in. Without it, you'll be no oil painting! Remember, your bed is your sanctuary and the mirror reflection doesn't lie. Get enough sleep and you'll be forever the prettiest princess – otherwise, be prepared to look like a potato face!

- You'll need about nine hours of sleep every night and it's important to make sure you get enough of it if you want to do well in your studies and in your sports. Starving yourself of these precious moments will leave you feeling sleepy, moody and with low concentration levels, plus it heightens your munchie attack potential because you'll be forced to look for foods to give you more energy.

- Avoid glugging back caffeine-filled tea and coffee to perk up your energy levels at the end of the day – this will really affect your sleep pattern later on, leaving you wide awake when you most need to sleep.

- To avoid waking up like a watermelon, sleep with your head on two pillows at night so that your face is up high. Never sleep face down, always sleep on your back, if you can. This prevents your face from looking puffy when you wake up – everything keeps circulating and fluid won't have settled.

- A great solution for getting a good night's sleep is to exercise regularly and don't eat dinner too late into the evening (you may need to discuss mealtimes with your mum).

- Late nights often result in puffy eyes. To de-puff them, pre-soak four teabags in iced water, lie back on your bed or the sofa and place over your eyelids. When they get warm after five minutes, switch them over with the other two teabags in the iced water and leave those on for a further ten minutes. Alternatively, try this process with fridge-chilled cucumber slices instead – chop up 4–6 slices and switch them when they get warm. It's a cheap and easy way to instantly soothe your peepers.

- Snoring our heads off at night, we actually lose a lot of our bodily fluids and this results in dehydrated skin and a dry throat. To prevent this happening, put a large glass of water by your bed to rehydrate the atmosphere and quench your skin.

- Doing exams can be tiring and draining, so, if you've been studying hard and you wake up in the morning with puffy eyes, try my apple surprise. Peel and core about six apples of your choice and pop them on a dry baking sheet in the oven at 140 degrees until they go super-soft-looking (this usually takes about 20 minutes). Ask your mum to help out if you can't navigate around the oven dial. Blend the roasted apple, squidge it around the eyes, lie back on your bed, leave for 15 minutes and then rinse off with warm water.

- Another way to get rid of 'studying' eye puffiness is to gently tap your fingers around your eye sockets for about 15 seconds. You can do this easy ritual every day. I do mine at night, after I have just washed my face.
- Studying and spending a lot of time at the computer can really take its toll and create huge bags under your eyes. If this is the case, just cut a couple of cold cucumber slices and place them over your eye sockets. Leave for ten minutes to refresh and relax your eyes.
- Is the central heating on full blast in the winter while you're asleep? If the answer's yes, just pop a glass or a bowl of water beside or under your radiator. This will help re-hydrate the dry atmosphere and therefore your skin too.
- To make your face look fresh and fab, splash cold water on to it in the morning. This stimulates circulation and brings a healthy glow to your complexion, plus it makes you appear more awake.
- Banish those bags from under your eyes with ice-cold spoons! Put two metal spoons in the freezer for 15 minutes and then hold them on the bags for about 20 seconds. Repeat on each bag five times.

HOW TO HAVE GLOWING SKIN

OK, so there are so many spots stuck to your face you might as well offer them up as the topping ingredients for a pepperoni and cheese pizza! Yep, those mini mountains have a nasty habit of appearing at the wrong time, zapping your confidence. So, I'm going to show you how to break free of those pesky little blighters. Get your eyeballs stuck into my secret skin remedies and, before you know it, you'll be picking and squeezing the hottest boy in town!

So, what are zits? Well, to start with, everybody gets them

and I mean everyone! They are commonly caused by normal hormonal fluctuations in your body and may be found on your back, scalp, face and neck. They can make you feel self-conscious, plus they're sometimes really uncomfortable. Although they might irritate you, don't be tempted to pick and squeeze – they can leave you with terrible scars. The more you irritate your spots, the more they will hurt and you'll only encourage them to spread, so don't let them win!

- Try not to touch money and then your face and especially not your mouth. Money is filthy and goes from one person to the next, passing on bacteria. Always wash your hands after touching it.
- Ask your mum if you can change the pillowcase on your bed every two days. Quite a lot of grease from your hair can build up on it. Sleep one night on the front, the next on the back and then change it.
- To zap the first signs of an angry-looking cold sore, press an ice cube on it for 15 minutes. To kill it off in the final stages, apply a mixture of ½ teaspoon lemon juice and ½ teaspoon salt. It hurts, but it works! Oh and remember... no kissing the boys till it has cleared up. You don't want to make it spread any further or, worse still, give one to the boy you have kissed! Somehow I don't think he will thank you for that.
- Mobile phones and landlines can be crawling with dirt and germs – bacteria just love to breed there! Every time you hold a phone up to your face, you are transferring germs. Every so often give your phone a wipe with an anti-bacterial cloth to get rid of them.
- Rather than picking greasy red zits, wrap an ice cube in a clean sock and hold it to the area for a minute or two. If you

are going straight out, dab some tea tree oil on it, leave to absorb, then cover with a light coating of concealer.

- Want to fight those greasy oily pimples while you sleep? Dab a blob of toothpaste on any spots to dry them up. It's quick, effective and cheap. But don't answer the door to the postman the next morning without washing the toothpaste off first or you'll give them the fright of their lives! I should know...

- Now I bet you never thought there would be a link between helping your mum by carrying the groceries home and a gorgeous glowing complexion. Well, there is! If you carry home the food for the week and work up a good old sweat, not only will you be helping blood to pump round your body faster and more efficiently, feeding your organs with vital nutrients and oxygen, but your mum will love you for doing it. Serious brownie points there!

- To remove blackheads, blitz up a bunch of fresh parsley in the blender for a few seconds (or ask a parent to help you do this) and massage on to the affected area. Leave the mush to work for about 15 minutes and then rinse off with warm water. Parsley is one of those wonderful little ingredients that nature created to make us look beautiful – a great cleanser.

- A facial massage will help stimulate the blood circulation in your face and flush out those nasty old toxins that cause spots. You can do this yourself at home with your own face cream, just massage gently in upward strokes.

- If a spot is about to erupt, clean your hands thoroughly and put a hot wet flannel over it to open up the pores. Now gently pull the skin away on either side of it (this should help to pop a ripe whitehead). Try to avoid squeezing as you will break and damage the skin. Rinse with cold water to close the pores back up.

- Lemon juice is brilliant for getting rid of blackheads! Rub the juice on to them before you go to bed, leave overnight and then rinse off in the morning. Continue doing this each night until all the blackheads have magically disappeared.

- Keeping your creams clean is really important. That's why it's better to buy pump-dispensers rather than big pots. After a while your pot of cream can become quite contaminated, especially if you keep dipping your paws in it without having washed them beforehand!

- Take one cod liver oil capsule every day for glowing skin. I wouldn't recommend taking it in liquid form on a teaspoon – it will make you want to hurl, believe me! Ask your mum if she's OK with this and if she wouldn't mind getting the capsules for you.

- Fresh air is one of the best beauty products out there. Plus you don't have to pay a single penny for it!

- If you lean on your hand while watching TV or when you're on your computer, make sure your hands are thoroughly clean, otherwise the dirt will go straight from your mitts to your face.

- Walking around town can make you feel really grubby, especially if you're out on a girly shopping spree and trying on clothes. When you get home, the first thing you should do is cleanse your face to prevent a sudden outbreak of spots. Wash as normal, then cut a couple of grapes in half and rub them all over your face (remove the pips first!). Rinse with cold water and moisturise. Grapes are a natural cleanser.

- Eat at least five or even six portions of fruit and vegetables a day to encourage your skin to glow.

- For a last-minute, fix-it job, cleverly placed concealer is a great way to hide a whitehead, but don't go splodging it on with your fingers, especially if the spot is freshly open and picked. Your hands could be carrying dirt, thereby transferring germs straight to your spot, which will then re-infect it. Instead, use a clean cotton bud to dab the concealer on.

- Trying to cover a scabby, crumbly spot with concealer can end up looking like a mini fruit crumble on your face, making it mega-obvious that you want to cover something up! What you need to do is to soften it up first. Dab a little Vaseline on it. Once this has been absorbed, apply a thin layer of concealer (it will now glide on), then a quick dusting of face powder to hold it all in place.

- So, you wake up in the morning, take a peek in the mirror and to your horror your face and neck have been attacked overnight by spots. What do you do? Well, a great way to treat them is cover unwelcome spots in carrot. Put a raw carrot in a kitchen blender (or ask a parent to help you) and apply to your skin. Leave for 20 minutes and rinse off. The carrot is great for calming down angry-looking spots and it will help to speed up the drying process.

CHEEKY LITTLE BOTTOM ZITS

Just because your pert little peaches are behind you and tucked away in your knickers, this doesn't mean you should neglect them. Like your face, they need lots of attention and TLC. Here are my tips.

- If you can't wait until you get home and have to use a public toilet, take a deep breath before you go in and think 'strong'. Rather than sitting on a germ-infested seat, cover the rim with lots of toilet roll (keep some tissues in your bag just in case you get caught out). Not only will this nicely cushion your little cream buns, it will also save contact with all those dreaded germs, which means it will also help you stay zit-free.

- Once a month, treat your bottom to a facial. Combine one tablespoon honey with the flesh of a ripe avocado (mash first) in a bowl. Smear it over your chirpy cheeks. Leave for 25 minutes and then rinse off. You can do all of this while standing up in the shower to avoid getting it all over the place.
- Exfoliate your bum once a week with exfoliating gloves to remove all dead skin cells and leave a glossy derrière.
- Avoid picking and squeezing bum zits – you'll only spread the germs and infect the area further. Leave them to dry out.
- If a spot is giving you grief, put an ice cube on it to take down the swelling. Cover the ice cube in a thin piece of cloth or tea-towel and hold it up against the spot for ten minutes. If you can't see what you're doing, sit on the edge of your bed and use a little hand mirror.
- You can, of course, spritz a little perfume on to any whiteheads as this will help them dry up. Boy, won't they smell nice, too!
- If you're hitting the beach and your bum is plastered in acne, slap on a layer of fake tan. This will disguise them a bit, plus you can wear shorts-style bikini bottoms that cover everything or even a little sarong.
- Finally, I hope you do this anyway, but make sure you wear clean knickers every day! Cotton knicks are always the best as they help to keep everything fresh down there.

KEEP ORANGE PEEL IN THE KITCHEN!

Instead of getting the bus to school, walk! Put your trainers on and stash smart school or work shoes in your bag (simply swap them when you get there). I can't emphasise enough how good exercise is for banishing cellulite. If your school isn't within walking distance, do something else that's active, such as washing the family car, sweeping up leaves in the garden or running up and down the stairs for ten minutes each. Never use an escalator either. Here are some more tips to banish that orange peel.

- Don't just wolf down your food as if someone's about to take it away from you. Not only will you look like a hog in full swing but the less you chew your food the more chances you have of forming cellulite and getting indigestion too. Chew, chew, chew, chicks!
- Coffee is a major culprit when it comes to cellulite so when you've brewed up a cup in the morning, rather than drinking it, transfer it to a bowl. Now jump in your empty bath and massage it into the affected areas to exfoliate, then rinse thoroughly.
- One of the most effective ways to get rid of the orange-peel effect from your thighs and bum cheeks is dry-brushing the skin using a natural bristle body brush. With firm strokes work all over your body in circular movements up towards the heart – this helps stimulate the blood flow and the lymphatic system.
- Exfoliating and massaging your body in the shower is another good way to combat cellulite. Massage on a daily basis and only ever exfoliate once or twice a week so as not to zap your skin of its natural oils.
- Believe it or not, stress can be a major cause of cellulite. When we're feeling anxious about something, we take short breaths and this encourages poor circulation, which can then lead to your skin not functioning properly and

valuable water being lost. Try and chill out, whether it's enjoying a relaxing bath, watching a funny DVD with your best mate, going to the cinema, taking a long walk with the dog (you can always borrow one!) and simply taking long, slow deep breaths.

- A lack of shut-eye, whether it's because you're stressed out about something or maybe you're a bit of a party chick and go to bed late on a regular basis, can also cause unsightly dimples.

- For a cellulite-free body, eating the right foods (especially raw foods, not meat) is essential. Overcooked food, especially vegetables, loses a lot of the goodness. Talk to your mum about this and maybe rescue the veg before it gets cooked into a mush. You can, of course, enjoy raw vegetable or fruit smoothies. Some of my top ingredients are pears (great for detoxifying – they contain high natural vitamins, fibre and lots of antioxidants, which basically give your body a new lease of life), watermelon (fab for combating water retention when you get your period and feel mega-bloated) and oats (an excellent fat-buster).

- Shovel in greenery like it's going out of fashion! Kale, watercress and broccoli should be your best friends from now on. Avocado is also great for keeping cellulite at bay.

- Finally, to get rid of that orange-peel look, try cutting down on sugar. If you do manage to cut down on your sugar content, and your cellulite does disappear, then bear in mind that, if you start eating sugary things again, your dreaded orange peel will return!

BANISH BOG BREATH

It might sound odd, but saliva is your best weapon against bad breath. Saliva helps wash away bacteria and food particles.

That's why you should carry some sugar-free gum with you at all times. It helps stimulate saliva production, which has antiseptic in it and this will help kill off bacteria, leaving you with fresher breath.

Now a lot of people think that blowing into cupped hands is a good indicator as to whether or not you have bad breath, but what they don't realise is that this is not an accurate test because we become accustomed to our own smells. If you want to do a little test, run a length of unflavoured dental floss through your upper and lower teeth at the back, then wait 50 seconds and smell it. If it doesn't smell of anything, you're fine, but if it smells of anything else, then I'm afraid so too does your breath! Another way of testing it is to lick the back of a clean wrist, wait 50 seconds and take a whiff of it. Here are some more tips to keep your breath smelling sweet!

- Often, bad breath originates from the tongue because of all the food that is left there. Each time you clean your teeth, scrub away at your tongue too with your toothbrush and a little toothpaste.
- If you've been scoffing stinky old garlic, chew on some parsley for as long as you can bear it. Parsley contains a chemical called chlorophyll, which zaps away smelly breath.
- Eat a handful of grapes to take a pungent smell away.
- Chew fresh mint or a minty chewing gum.
- Floss your teeth every day. Old food loves to sneak its way in between your teeth, which can create bad breath.
- Eat a small pot of live natural yoghurt – live yoghurt is jam-packed with good bacteria that can fight the smell-inducing bad bacteria.
- Make sure a visit to your dentist or hygienist to get your teeth and gums professionally cleaned is put to the top of

your to-do list about twice a year. I'm sure your parents sort out these check-ups anyway but, if not, ask them to book you in.

- If you are the owner of a removable brace, wash it thoroughly before putting it back in your mouth. Soak it in some warm water for a few minutes, then, using toothpaste on your toothbrush, simply brush away as you would your teeth. Rinse with cold running water.

- Never hit the sack if you haven't brushed your teeth. Not only will you wake up smelling like you swallowed your dad's cheesy socks but it's also really unhealthy for your teeth not to be cleaned of all the food that you have consumed that day. That's when tooth rot sets in!

- I'm a huge fan of antibacterial mouthwashes. After you've brushed your teeth, just swizzle the stuff around in your mouth for about 30 seconds. It freshens your breath and helps to fight decay while you sleep.

PUT A SMILE ON YOUR FACE!

A big whopper of a smile, beaming from ear to ear, is one of the best accessories a girl can have, and it doesn't matter how nice a person you might be, yellowing little rat teeth are a sure way of making people try their hardest to steer you away from fun and giggly conversations on to more serious, even sad ones in a desperate attempt to get you to keep your mouth shut! Here are some tips to help your smile.

- Change your toothbrush regularly. Over time, they become bent and useless but they can also become contaminated with little food pieces and eventually start to ferment.

- Ease off on the penny sweets and any other sugary foods that love to rot and decay your pegs.

- To make brushing my teeth go more quickly, I watch TV at the same time!

- If you want to step it up a gear and get the ultimate tooth-cleaning experience, ask your mum to buy you an electric toothbrush. Once you've tried one, there will be no looking back. Plus they're really good fun!

- Despite regular brushing, food can easily become trapped in between our teeth, but dental floss will remove it from its cosy little holes. This in turn will sweeten your breath, plus you'll be saving your parents a fortune at the dentist because you won't have to book yourself in for extra fillings.

- If you enjoy a cup of tea, try not to make it too strong. Tea really stains your teeth and, over time, they can start to look like sweetcorn kernels! If, however, they are already a bit yellowy-looking, try this little old-fashioned treatment: dampen your toothbrush, dip it in some baking soda and brush your teeth as usual. Baking soda is renowned for removing stains and whitening teeth, plus it's dead cheap.

- Buy one of those little pots with lots of holes at the top to hold your toothbrush. Germs can transfer from one brush to the other, which often leads to infections and the pot will keep them separate so they won't cross-contaminate.

- Don't be scared of the dentist – he or she is there to help you look as lovely as possible! Regular visits will keep dentures at bay, too.

- Grated lemon zest is fantastic for whitening your teeth (good news for those who like fizzy drinks). Simply rub it over them and after a few tries the stained colour will start to fade.

- Finally, make sure you rinse your toothbrush thoroughly under running water every time you use it. For ultimate hygiene, change it every two months too.

HAPPY HOLIDAYS

It's your call: you can look like a sun-kissed Brazilian babe parading down the beach in your gorgeous Sienna Miller-style dress, all hot and hippy, or more like you're meant to be on a Mediterranean menu – yes, a fresh red lobster. Ouch!

Some girls frazzle themselves to a crisp, convinced the blistering pinkness will turn to brown the next day, and that burning the skin is nothing to worry about. Well, think again! In fact, the sun can be very ageing and too much of it can even lead to skin cancer in extreme cases. But I'm not saying you need to spend the rest of your life shut away in a dark room, looking so pasty you could be mistaken for a ghost – it's totally cool to spend time under the lovely rays of the sun, provided you slap on the high-factor cream, drink lots of water and be sensible.

SO, WHO'S MOST AT RISK?

Anyone with lots of moles, those who find it really hard to tan in the first place, anyone who burns really easily, even with a high factor on and those who have fair skin and hair. And if you think your moles look different to normal or they have started to itch, I strongly advise you to make an appointment with your doctor as soon as possible to have them checked out.

YOUR SUN-CREAM DOSSIER

- So, why use sun cream? Firstly, it helps to filter out harmful UV rays that cause skin cancer and premature ageing. To really protect your skin, go for a cream with a really high factor. The following tips will also help you make the most of the sun.
- Apply a new layer of sun cream every two hours. If you're in and out of the water like a Jack-in-the-Box, apply every

hour and opt for a water-resistant formula. It won't wash off and will stick to your skin for as long as possible. Water-resistant is also good if you're a bit of a Sweaty Betty!

- Never store sun creams for more than a year. They will offer your skin no protection at all. Check the sell-by date and always sniff your cream to see if it still smells fresh. Buy fresh ones each year so they do their job properly every time.

- Never scrimp when putting on sun cream. Spoon it on if you have to, like Jamie Oliver would add cream to a Pavlova!

- Try not to go out in the sun and then apply your sun cream. Instead, do it 30 minutes beforehand so it has a chance to thoroughly absorb into your skin.

- Now getting to those difficult areas on your back can be really hard sometimes unless you have spaghetti-like arms (very useful in this case!), so ask a friend (or parent) to do this for you — otherwise you may end up with some embarrassing-looking red splodges on your back. Believe me, they won't look good with your little pretty frock!

- Vitamin D is one of the good guys for our bods. It's vital for our bones, teeth, skin, weight management, sleep pattern, good digestion and eye health. Vitamin D protects our bodies making sure they function properly. Without it, your body may suffer as it will lack the help it needs to keep in tip-top condition. We get vitamin D from sunlight, but don't go toasting yourself too much! Just four minutes of sunshine is enough for our daily quota.

MORE SUNBATHING TIPS

- Try not to spend the whole day in the sun. Morning and late afternoon are the best and safest times to be out and about. From 11.30am till 3pm, try to stay in the shade as the sun is at its strongest.

- Looking lobster red means those harmful UV rays that come jetting out of the atmosphere from above have damaged your skin cells. If you keep doing this when you are outside and not protecting yourself from the sun, this can cause long-term damage to your skin. It means you will get wrinkles at an early age and, on a more serious note, it increases your chances of getting skin cancer. So, please, put sun-protection cream on and stay safe.

- If you feel yourself burning, stick to the shade or pop on a T-shirt.

- If you've taken a quick dip in the water with your T-shirt on (so Miami!), then keep in mind that the fibres may stretch, allowing little UV rays to sneak in through your top and burn your skin. Opt for T-shirts made of natural fibres, such as cotton and linen – they won't stretch as much as manmade. If your wet top has stretched, then take it off and put a dry one on. That way those naughty little UV guys won't be able to work their way in quite so much.

- If you like to spend a lot of time in the sun, wear a thin T-shirt to help keep the harmful rays out, but leave you cool and comfortable at the same time.

- Don't forget to apply sun-protection cream to all those odd little areas of your body, such as your ears, the soles of your feet and the backs of your knees.

- If you're in a tropical country (or even Europe) and the sky is full of clouds, don't be deceived: harmful sunrays can still push their way through – you might not be able to see them but, trust me, they are still there big time. So, don't forget to slap on a layer of cream.

- If the Olsen twins do it, then so can we… Hats, hats, hats! Not only do they keep your style status high, but they also protect your face from the harmful sun.

- Don't think that, because you're in the water, you won't burn. Harmful UV rays filter their way through water and can still burn you. Use a waterproof cream and remember to reapply it every few hours.

- Some people think that using a sun bed isn't at all dangerous. Wrong! The UV rays in a sun bed can be ten times stronger than the natural sun! So avoid them at all costs.

- Sunglasses are a must in the sun. Not just because they protect your eyesight from the sun and prevent wrinkles landing on your face at a young age (you won't be screwing your eyes up), but because you can also check out the talent from behind them without ever being detected!

- To keep you cool by the pool, fill a little spray bottle with water and spritz your face every so often. Also, don't forget to take a bottle of water to drink so that you don't become dehydrated.

- Always carry baby wipes with you. They're so useful for cleaning sticky sun-cream mitts and fingers before you eat!

FABULOUSLY FAKE!

Channel your inner goddess with a DIY fake tan. Yep, no streaks and no stains – it's time to fake a flawless tan and be a bronzed beauty. Here's how.

- Put on a pair of exfoliating gloves and gently remove all the dead skin cells from your face and body (pay particular attention to the elbows, knees and ankles, which can often be dry). This will help you apply the tan evenly without it sticking to any dry patches.

- Now, give your skin a drink! Moisturise it up (especially the naturally dry bits, such as elbows and knees) until it's silky smooth. Look for a moisturiser that isn't too oily to allow the fake tan to absorb properly, preventing it from clogging and clutching dry bits.

- Never apply too much fake tan at once. Your skin can only absorb a certain amount and too much can result in nasty streaks.

- Now squirt a blob of fake tan on to your palms and work it into your face. Make sure you work upwards towards the hairline. Be careful not to get tan into the hair itself or you'll look as if you missed your mouth having curry last night and it ended up in your hair! If you're worried about getting it in your locks, rub a thin line of Vaseline into the edge of your hairline and this will prevent the fake tan from sticking to your hair.

- If you can't reach tricky areas such as your back, ask your mum to help out.

- Never apply fake tan to your eyebrows. Seriously, if you do, don't be surprised if people giggle at you. Your brows will be orangey brown! If you think your hands might wobble, smear a tiny bit of Vaseline on to your brows and this will prevent them from clogging up.

- Go carefully over your knees, ankles and elbows – just a light sweep of tan here will do.

- Make sure you don't forget to smear a little fake tan down your neck, otherwise you'll risk looking like a brown lollipop on top of a pale stick!

- Don't forget to fake tan your earlobes, too – a light covering, mind! Two little white earlobes sticking out of a brown face isn't a good look.

- Don't bypass your armpits – they can often be on show and look dreadful, if they're left white.

- If you're low on fake-tan lotion and can't get to the shops, then fake it and fill in the bits that are visible to the eye. So, if your arms and ankles will be on show, just do those bits and leave the rest white. How naughty is that? I do it all the time. Make sure you don't forget the next day and put on a short skirt to reveal white legs and brown ankles, though!

- To preserve your newly sun-kissed look, pat your skin dry after a shower and apply lots of lovely moisturiser.
- If and when you see an area that looks as if it could do with a touch-up, scrub that patch and then apply a new lick of fake tan just to that area.
- And finally, all you bronzed beauties, always wash your hands carefully afterwards! Because towels often get trashed by fake-tan lotion, ask your mum if she could kindly donate an old towel to you for faking. Or you can always use the dog's if you get desperate! You'd better ask him too, though!

STOP SNACKING ON YOUR NAILS – HOW TO HAVE LOVELY HANDS

Bitten nails isn't a good look for any Lazy Princess in the making, so if you can't keep the stumps out of your mouth and you long to be the owner of a set of lovely long talons just like Cheryl Cole's, drastic action is needed! Here's what to do.

- First, buy yourself some of that anti-nail-biting varnish and spread it over your nails and cuticles (where your nails and skin meet). The taste is so revolting that it will soon deter you from putting your nails anywhere near your mouth!
- I understand that biting your nails can become a habit, one that's really hard to give up. So, rather than going cold turkey and trying to stop biting your nails overnight, try to limit your biting to one hand only and leave the other hand well alone. After a week, limit the fingers that you can chew

on (cut out your thumb and your little finger to leave just three others to chew on). Then, after another week, limit it to just one finger, then, three days later, stop biting that one too. See how your other nails have all grown to a lovely length and, by now, you will have hopefully broken the habit.

- False nails that stick on top of your existing ones are a great way to help keep your fingers away from your mouth – you won't want to ruin your new look, plus you won't be able to get anywhere near the real nails. Make sure you check with your parents and the school first.
- Always keep your nails clean. Every time you wash them, scrub the underneath too with a nailbrush.
- A really strongly scented hand cream should stop you from chewing your nails.
- Always keep a nail file with you at all times so that, if you do jag a nail, you can file it away at once instead of biting it.
- Dip your nails in a little cup of olive oil for eight minutes each night to soften the cuticles (and stop you munching on them).
- If you need to open a box or an envelope, use a pair of scissors, not your nails.

A-LIST YOUR NAILS

It still amazes me how many chicks will spend hours shopping for, and putting together a really cool outfit only to ruin the whole look with chipped and chewed nails and rough hands. They say your hair is your crowning glory, but I think nails are even more so. They're one of the first things that people notice about you and I'm sorry, but your gorgeous twinkly rings don't deserve to be carried around on monster munch mitts! So, arm yourself with a nail file and put an end to your biting now! It's time to treat yourself to a manicure.

- If you want a cheat's version of a French manicure without actually doing it, just paint the ends of your nails in white.
- Another good high-maintenance fake French mani is to buy a white nail pencil from a beauty desk and apply it under the nail. It takes about a minute to do this, costs next to nothing and looks very convincing indeed! How's that for ultra-lazy?
- Who said French manicures only ever have white tips? How about doing neon pink? Yum!
- If you wear dark nail polish, always keep your nail colour in your bag – chipped nails are positively scabby-looking! If you need to remove the polish and you're on the bus, say, then you can buy pre-soaked remover pads that do the job in one, meaning you don't have to carry a bottle of remover around with you.
- Always keep a mini nail file board in your bag so that as soon as you get a snag you can deal with it, rather than having it irritate you so much you munch it right down to the cuticle!
- Used next to your nails, dark nail varnishes can start to stain them yellow after a while. To prevent this, apply a layer of base coat beforehand, then a couple of layers of your dark colour.
- Never file your nails in a zig-zag motion. Instead, go from left to right. This will stop you snagging them and weakening them in the process.
- To remove yellow stains from your nails, rub them with lemon juice. Over time, they will disappear.
- People who smoke cigarettes will often have two or three yellow-looking nails, as the nicotine in the ciggies will discolour them. How rank is that? So, girlies, be sensible and stay well away from the nasty little sticks! They're terrible for your health, plus they play havoc with your natural beauty.

Treat Yourself to a Cheryl Cole-Style Manicure!

Any diva in the making needs to make sure her nails are in tippy top condition. If you want an A-list treatment at a fraction of the price, follow the tips below.

- Always remove old nail varnish first.
- Massage some Vaseline into your cuticles to soften them up. Now fill two cereal bowls halfway up with warm soapy water and dip your nails in it for 10 to 15 minutes.
- Using a nailbrush gently scrub away all the dirt. Pat your hands dry with a towel and then, using a cuticle stick, clean all the trapped dirt from underneath your nails.
- Next, push your cuticles away from your nails. To do this, use the flat edge of your cuticle stick. Not only will this make your nails instantly look better and longer, it will also help them grow more quickly.
- Wash your hands with a dash of washing-up liquid under running water and dry thoroughly.
- Now it's time to shape your nails (square or rounded) with your nail file. Square looks, and is, more high maintenance whereas a rounded shape is a little more low-key, yet it doesn't chip quite so easily. Don't leave any rough edges – these will snag on your clothes and could result in further biting. Only ever file in one direction for a split-free, perfect finish.

- Now wash and dry your hands. It's time to apply the nail polish of your choice. Shake the bottle first and then use three to four brush strokes per nail. Any more and you may end up with a messy streaked look.
- Sit somewhere cool for at least 20 minutes to allow your nails to dry.

- Look for nail polishes that come with short brushes – they are so much easier to use. Long brushes can often result in you putting too much polish on your nails, which ends up looking super-gooey and messy.
- Ten minutes before you apply your nail polish, pop it in the fridge. This will make it go on more easily and you will therefore use less and save a bit of money in the long run.
- If you are in a rush, but still want to paint your nails, then buy polishes that dry in 60 seconds. There's nothing worse than smudged talons.
- When painting your divine little nails with colour, apply the polish 2mm away from the cuticle for a straight-out-of-the-salon look.
- I paint my nails rather like I butter my toast! Start from the outside in for even coverage all over. It's the same when it comes to painting your nails – I start from the edges of the nail tips to 2mm away from the cuticles. Why? Not only does this prevent them from chipping straight away, but it also makes the polish more hardwearing.
- Nail-proof your mitts with multicolour nail varnish. Paint each one in a completely different colour. Perfect for a party!
- Freshly painted nails always take twice as long to dry in a

warm place. If you need them to dry quickly, go somewhere cold or get your hair dryer out and put it on the cold setting to blast them dry.

- Dark nail polish that is chipped and chewed looks terrible, so take it off all together and go nude until you're reunited with your polish.
- Try to avoid filing your nails while they are covered in polish. This will only weaken them.
- For added shine, always apply a topcoat to your coloured nail varnish.
- Try not to get nail varnish on your cuticles – you'll not only dry them out, but you'll also prevent them from growing properly.

HEAVENLY HANDS AND NAILS

- Always have a tube of hand cream close by at all times so that you can give your hands a good old top-up as and when. I've got lots of mini tubes scattered all over the house! I carry one in my handbag and I have one by each of my sinks and one in the drawer by the bed.
- If you're helping your parents with any heavy DIY work, always wear rubber gloves to protect your mitts.
- Use a facemask on dry chapped hands to re-nourish and feed your poor little mitts.
- If your mum's nagging has worked and you're tied to the kitchen sink doing the washing up, make sure you wear rubber gloves. Household cleaning products or detergents can be very harsh, and I can tell you this, your new Cheryl Cole French mani won't thank you! Washing-up liquids can make the skin around your nails all flaky and dry – not very WAG! Now you can even get washing-up liquid that conditions your hands and stops them from drying out!

How annoying is that? There's no getting out of the washing up now…

- When you're out in the sun, slather sun-protection cream on your hands.

- If you want stronger nails, eat lots of sugar-free jelly. The gelatine in it is great for keeping your nails, hair and bones strong. You can do as I do and eat one cube a day straight out of the packet, or you can do it tea-party style and make a proper jelly with lovely fresh fruits. It is a healthy low-fat treat to have every day and is a fun way to help towards your five-a-day fruit intake.

- I always used to have dried flaky skin around my nails and I pretty much spent the whole day gnawing away on it! To get rid of it, squeeze the tips of your fingers for ten seconds every day. What this does is stimulate the blood circulation. It can be a bit boring, so I do mine while I'm watching TV!

- You'd be surprised how much dirt can get stuck underneath a pretty ring, so take it off each day (not above the sink, though!), wash your hands and replace your ring.

- While filming *60 Minute Makeover* for ITV1, I must have got about a log's worth of wooden splinters stuck somewhere in my fingers, I joke you not! A clever builder on the show gave me the best tip to get rid of them. Just cover your fingers in greasy hand cream or Vaseline and leave to soak overnight. During the night, your skin will become mega-soft, which eventually encourages the splinter to work its way out.

- Another way to remove splinters is to numb the area with an ice cube and then remove the darned thing using a pair of tweezers. Ask your mum or dad to lend a hand.

- If your nails have white polka dots on them (and I don't

mean those fake nail extensions that you apply!), your body might be short of zinc, so eat lots of pumpkin seeds.

- Perhaps you're a bit of a whizz kid in the kitchen, but fed up with your hands stinking of onion. If so, try this trick. Once the onion has been pieced open and the skin is off, shove it under running water. This will take most of the toxic fumes away, which can make your eyes water like crazy. To remove the stench from your mitts, rub the flesh of a lemon on to your hands for a few minutes and then rinse with water. You can do the same after handling garlic. Lemon is great for cleansing your hands and taking bad smells away.

- If you've been busy building dens in the back-garden bushes all day, all those twigs and thorns may leave you with hands that look and feel like sandpaper. To bring them back to their usual smooth self, get a handful of porridge oats, soak them in a dash of warm water from the tap, mix and lather up in the palm of your hands. Your hands will absorb the vitamin E from the oats, which will nourish your mitts, and the fibre helps to remove dead skin cells. You can also use a tablespoon of brown sugar with a dot of olive oil and scrub

Becci Ireland – *Fashion and Beauty Editor of MIZZ Magazine*

A tiny tub of Vaseline is a handbag must-have. It's great for applying to irritating dry patches, cracked lips, nasty cuticles or even for tidying up messy eyebrows.

this into the palms of your hands over the sink. It's also great for softening the skin.

- How many times have you picked up a pen, only to discover that it leaks all over your hands? Well, I've got just the thing to get rid of it – and it's in your fruit basket. Simply cut a lemon in half and rub the fleshy side over the ink stain for a minute. Wash your hands with soap, dry and then moisturise them with hand cream.

SWEET FEET

If you're getting strange looks from people, your feet might just stink of cheese! If this is the case, fear not ...

- If your feet really pong, ask your mum if you can have some of her baking soda and sprinkle it on them to keep some of the smell at bay for a while. Oh, and don't forget to sprinkle some of this magic dust into your smelly shoes too. Leave overnight and vacuum it out in the morning.
- Another good way of attacking the cheesy feet situation is to soak your feet in a lemon mix. Simply squeeze six lemons and add the juice to a big mug of warm water. Mix and then transfer to a shallow dish. Pop your feet in, turn on the TV, then sit back and relax for 20 to 30 minutes.
- If your tootsies feel like sandpaper, it's time to soften them up. Warm up a cup of olive oil in the microwave until it's comfortably hot (or ask your mum to help you with this). Ask your mum if you can borrow a shallow cooking dish or basin of some sort, one that's large enough to fit your feet in. Pour the olive oil into the dish, pop your trotters in and leave for 20 minutes. Before you take them out, make sure you've rubbed the oil into every part of your feet.
- To stop piggy toes from rubbing together just after you've

painted them, roll up a long strip (or individual strips) of cotton wool and quickly weave it in and out of each toe. You can also use plastic toe separators but cotton wool works just as well.

- If you suffer from ingrowing toenails, use sharp scissors to cut a V shape in the centre of the nail at the top to force the sides to grow inwards again, relieving the outer-edge skin.
- Toe rings look cute, but only if you keep them clean!
- Paint your nails in one cool and funky colour, allow to dry and then paint some dots on top of them. For instance, red toes go well with white dots, or orange with blue dots. You could also do stripes – it's so easy and looks rockin'!

LOOK AFTER YOUR BODY

- If you have trouble trying to reach those difficult parts on your back to give it a good old scrub, get a pair of old tights, chop one leg off and pop a bar of soap halfway down inside it. Tie a knot either side of the soap, then simply throw it over your shoulder and scrub away! You'll notice how all the dead skin comes loose and sticks to the tights. Lovely!
- Those little spot-like bumps on the backs of your arms could well be fatty deposits. They are very easy to get rid of – just exfoliate daily with your bristly body brush.
- Do you wake up some mornings feeling like a beached whale because you haven't done a poo in ages? Well, you've got constipation. So, drink a cup of boiling water with a third of the juice of a lemon and a dollop of honey first thing in the morning, about 45 minutes before you have your breakfast, each day.
- To make your skin as cuddly as your softest teddy, put three tablespoons of powered milk in your bath, then lie back and

relax. This helps get rid of dead skin cells, plus it's the perfect excuse to zoom off into fantasy land thinking about your hot crush!

PERFECT PINS

Some lucky girls are born with the most amazing long legs that just seem to go on forever and ever, way past their armpits, and look so irritatingly good in a pair of skinny jeans with flat shoes. Then there are the girls who aren't so lucky, the ones born with cut-off tree stumps! Whatever category you are, here are a few helpful hints to make your pins look more like a stretch limo.

- A little light dusting of shimmer powder down the middle of your shins creates the illusion of muscle definition.
- If your legs are similar to corned beef hash (mottled) or spotty like salami slices, then a layer of fake tan will help to cover them up and even out your skin. Fake tan is especially good if you look whiter than white chalk and you want to look sun-kissed within hours. What's more, it's always better for your skin than sitting in the sun for days on end as it will reduce the risk of you getting skin cancer and slows down premature ageing.
- If your legs look a little bit like pizza (red, spotty and irritated) due to ingrown hairs (caused through shaving), then exfoliate them with your exfoliating gloves to remove the top layer of dead skin cells, which can trap the hair. When shaving, do so while your legs are wet. Anyway, what are ingrown hairs? Well, it's when hair grows out of the skin and then curls back in again to cause minor infections. Don't worry, though – with a bit of exfoliation on a daily basis those dreaded red spots are history!

- Keep your legs moisturised at all times to avoid the scaly fish look.
- Vertical striped tights are always more flattering to the leg, especially compared to horizontal stripes.
- For instantly healthier-looking legs, brush them with bronzing powder.
- To tone your legs up, always take the stairs, where possible. You'll be glad you did when it's the summer and you want to get your pins out in your little denim mini!

LOOKING AFTER YOUR LEGS

I've seen it, time after time: chicks looking Cheryl Cole cool. From a distance the picture of bespoke beauty with glossy manes flowing in the wind, stunning white nails and an utterly irresistible dress, only the whole look is ruined by an abundance of hair poking through fine silk stockings or tights. Shock, horror!

Did you know that shaving first became popular during World War II when the much-desired silk stockings were in short supply (as were all other luxuries) and the women had to shave their legs to mimic smooth, hairless legs? But not only that, they also used to use a thin mixture of gravy colouring or tea to stain their legs to make it look like they were wearing stockings. Another great little trick they had tucked up their sleeves was to draw a line up the back of their legs using eyeliner pencil to look like stocking seams. And why did they go to all of this effort? Because they wanted their legs to look sexy and alluring.

These days, your legs can still be the centre of attention, so make sure you put as much effort into making them look good as our lovely ladies did then. There are a few simple rules that you have to follow. So here's how to keep your legs looking lovely – and if all else fails, there's always the left-over gravy from your Sunday roast if things get desperate!

- Always exfoliate before you shave. This will get rid of the dead skin and prevent ugly ingrown hairs, plus it will give you a closer shave.
- Wet your skin beforehand. The heat from the water will soften the hair making it easier to remove.
- Don't use soap to shave your legs. Use a proper shaving foam or conditioner. Choose a smell that you love to make the experience a whole lot better.
- Look for a razor with a lubricant strip. As you are shaving, the strip leaves a line of juicy gel on your skin, meaning you aren't shaving dry skin, which can cause irritation. My favourite is Gillette Venus.
- Start shaving from the bottom of the ankle up towards your knee, going against the direction of hair growth. If you are shaving your armpits, you will need to shave in all directions as the hair there grows every which way.
- Always rinse your razor after every stroke to prevent the blade from clogging up with dead skin and hair.
- Be careful going around your ankles – this is where most of the cuts happen. Take your time!
- When the job is done and your legs are looking silky smooth, give them a good old moisturise for that glossy look. The skin on your legs has few oil glands so it needs all the help it can get to avoid looking dry and scaled.
- Change your razor regularly – the blade can become blunt after a time, which can result in cuts and infections.
- Don't ever share your razor with someone, however much you love them. It's unhygienic and sharing can cause skin irritations and infections.

- Another alternative to get rid of beastly hair is a hair removal cream (Veet is a great brand). It's the easiest thing in the world to use. You slap the stuff on with the little spatula that comes with it, wait for five minutes, then scrape off the cream, which brings the hair with it, and rinse yourself under a coldish shower.

- Waxing strips are good for smoothing those hairy, carpet-like legs. I personally find them a bit tricky and a little more painful, but they still do a very good job. With these, all you have to do is lay one at a time on to clean legs, smooth it down and rip off in the opposite direction of the hair growth. Ouch!

- If you want the whole beauty-salon experience, then hint at your mum and dad that it's something that you would love for your next birthday.

SHORTCUTS TO A BEAUTIFUL BARNET

There's nothing worse than having to wash your hair when you really can't be bothered – so, don't! Take the ultimate lazy-girl option and spray dry shampoo (from most chemists and supermarkets) into your hair. Leave for five seconds to absorb all the grease and then brush out. Hey presto, you'll look like you've just stepped out of the salon! Here are some more timesaving tips.

- If you haven't got time to wash your hair and it stinks like a drain, then spray a little bit of perfume into it – don't overdo it, though! You don't want anyone passing out.

- Sweep your hair back off your face and up into a ponytail. Don't brush it up – you'll only highlight the fact that you've got lard-like hair! Instead, rake your fingers through your locks to give a textured, non-greasy look. Also, having your hair up off your face helps prevent spots.

- To keep grubby hair out of your face, hold it up with the end of an old pair of tights. Cut the foot off and put it over your hair like a swimming hat. This is also a good little trick for when you are applying your face mask so that you don't get any of the gunk in your hair.
- Wear a hat or scarf on your head to disguise the grease.
- When you're in a hurry but your hair's horribly greasy, put it up into a loose bun. Pull forward as much or as little of the front section as you like and wash that bit under the sink tap. Dry as usual. The clean hair at the front gives the impression that the rest of your hair is lovely and clean, not dripping in grime.
- Another good way of camouflaging manky hair is to put sections in rollers, apply a little hairspray to them and leave for five seconds to dry. Gently remove the rollers so as not to break the hair. Your hair will now boast a rather voluminous Hollywood style.
- You can also give your barnet a little blast with the hairdryer to lift the roots and encourage more volume. You don't need to dampen it at all. Just blast it on the hot level, which will bring it back to life for a few hours more.

HOW TO ACHIEVE LUSTROUS LOCKS

- Olive oil isn't just for helping that stir-fry along, or making a salad yummy – it's also brilliant for making your hair glossier than the pages of *Vogue*! Simply rub some into the roots of your hair and leave it in for 15 minutes, then wash as normal with shampoo and conditioner. Do this once every two weeks.
- Dilute fresh lemon juice in a large container of lukewarm water (a roasting tin will do) and dunk your head in it. Rub the mixture into your scalp to stimulate hair growth. Lemon

juice is magic when it comes to making blonde hair zing with shine, plus it's great for removing dandruff.

- If you've run out of regular conditioner, substitute a soft fabric conditioner. This trick is also fine for those with sensitive skin.
- After you've washed your hair, always do the last rinse with cold water to encourage it to shine.
- If you've got more oil in your hair than you'd find in a chippie, you need a pampering session! Rub a mixture of warm water, a touch of salt and two teaspoons of vinegar into it and leave for a couple of hours. Rinse with cold water to keep the chippie effect at bay.
- Stuff your face with salmon on a regular basis (swizzled down with a glass of sparkling water on the rocks, of course!). The fish oils contained in it will nourish the cuticles of your hair, making it thicker and stronger.
- Hairbrushes can clog up with the grub and grease from your dirty hair, so give them a wash with shampoo every two weeks so you don't pass grease on to freshly washed locks.
- Massage your hair every time you wash it, to stimulate hair growth.

BAD HAIR DAYS

This tip is one I learned from experience when I was 17 and out in the middle of nowhere in Bali. My bleached-blonde hair decided to go radioactive green after I jumped into a heavily chlorinated swimming pool. Luckily, I had brought with me a stash of my must-have groceries, the ones that I literally can't live without: Earl Grey teabags being one of them and tomato ketchup, the other. It was my trusty ketchup that saved the day! I just squeezed a quarter of the bottle on to my damp hair, massaged it in and left it for ten minutes to neutralise the colour, then washed it out with shampoo and conditioned afterwards. For more troubleshooting tips, read on.

- To prevent coloured blonde hair from going green in the first place, simply cover damp hair in conditioner before you throw yourself into the pool to stop your hair from absorbing the chlorine.
- If the thought of wearing a swimming hat makes you cringe, yet you don't want to damage your blonde highlights, do the conditioner treatment above or wet it completely and pop it up into a bun. That way, your hair absorbs clear water first, reducing the amount of chlorine that will stick to your hair.
- If your blonde locks have been greedy and hoovered up lots of chlorine and your hair is now a rather scary shade of green, make a mixture of two cups of warm water and some vinegar. Rinse it over your hair. This won't remove all the green, but it will get rid of enough for you to make it safely to the hair salon without people laughing at you.
- If your hair has gone AWOL and is a bit frizzy, tame it down by smoothing a mini-blob of hand cream over the surface.
- Lightly dampen flat, limp hair with a garden-plant spray bottle filled with tap water, then stick your head upside down. Blow-dry while scrunching away for instant volume.
- Always carry a handbag-sized hairbrush and styling spray on you in case you get caught in the rain without a brolly. All you have to do is dash to the ladies' room and dry your hair under the hand-dryer.
- If your hair turns into a static Afro after you've blow-dried it, smooth it over with a silk scarf to remove flyaway hairs and to give a glossy finish.

- Alternatively, calm down uncontrollably static hair by spraying hairspray on to a brush and groom it from top to bottom.

- If your hair is beginning to morph into a matted-down Turkish rug, with more tangles than a bundle of Christmas tree lights, I've got just the solution. Wash your hair once, pat dry with a towel and then cake on loads of rich hair conditioner. Massage it in everywhere and leave for 30 minutes. Now, separate your hair strands with your fingertips, taking care not to split them (always work from the bottom upwards). When you feel like you've got rid of some of the knots, get a wide-toothed comb and gently work those knots out, again going from the bottom to the top. When all of the knots have gone, rinse the conditioner out or leave in for a few extra hours of moisturising.

- Always concentrate when your hairstylist is cutting your locks or you may end up with an Edward Scissorhands' creation that you absolutely hate! So, lay off the texting your mate or reading a magazine and, if you spot something you don't like, don't be afraid to ask them to stop and tell them what you'd prefer before it's too late.

SALON STYLE AT HOME

- Freshly washed hair is always harder to style – why? Because when you wash your hair, it leaves it all lovely and glossy, so it's a nightmare to arrange. So, if you're planning an up-do, then wash your hair the day before and it will have a lot more grip to it.

- If your hair is silky or a bit frizzy, then whack a bit of serum into it and this will give it that much-needed control.

- Funk up your tresses with some cute hair clips for instant evening glamour.

- Fancy Amy Winehouse's big bouffant? Set that hair comb of yours to work by backcombing it until it's skyscraper high, and hold it in place by simply blasting a bit of firm-hold hairspray into it.

- Wrap small sections of hair round non-heated curlers and, while you're waiting for them to set, soak away in a hot bath. The steam helps set and style your hair. Afterwards, give your hair a gentle blast with the hairdryer to ensure it's completely dry. Now you can gently remove the curlers, put some fix spray in it and, hey presto, a complete halo of curls!

- For lustrous curls, plait your hair in two French plaits down the side of your head and leave to dry. I sleep in mine and, when I wake up in the morning, I undo them and whack a bit of texture spray in them and scrunch it about.

- If you're still at school and want to show off your style status, do your hair differently every day. This is a great way of expressing yourself when you're not permitted to do so via your clothes. Rules are rules!

- If your beaded necklace falls apart, rather than throwing it out, keep it and tie it into your hair with a hair band to secure it in place.

- Spray dry locks with hairspray to help keep your style in place and give extra volume, when needed.

- Invest in a pair of hair-straightening irons – they'll help create a mega-hot, fresh-out-of-the-salon look, from cute curls to shiny straight. When your birthday or Christmas is nearing, start throwing out subtle hints for a pair.

- To create tumbling tresses, take 2.5cm-wide sections of damp hair and add mousse. Coil round your finger, clip to your head and blast with the hairdryer until dry. Take the hair clips out, jiggle the curls around gently, then blast a bit of fine hairspray to hold in place.

- A ponytail needn't be boring! In fact, if you've got long or medium-length hair, it can be a great template for some seriously cool looks. For example, scatter small fresh or plastic flowers in your hair, securing them with hair clips. Once your ponytail is secured in place, separate the actual tail into five sections, then put a band at the end of each one.
- Get your crimpers out and give your hair some fun!
- Make a homemade hairband from a small scarf or a scrap of unusual material, even a length of thin rope. Anything goes, really!

A LITTLE TLC FOR LUSH LOCKS

- After washing your hair, stick it in a homemade turban (this helps to soak up excess water). Leave to dry 75% (you can easily fill in the waiting time gossiping to a friend on the phone, putting on your make-up, or doing some homework) and then blow-dry it on a medium heat. Never blow-dry your hair when it's soaking wet or you will cause long-term damage by over-drying it. Plus, wet hair is very fragile and prone to breakages.
- You can do a bit of DIY hair-cutting anywhere. All you have to do is wrap a small piece of hair around your finger until the split end is visible, then snip it off with a pair of sharp scissors. Be careful, though.
- Eat your way to healthy hair with plenty of fruit, vegetables and protein to encourage your locks to grow. Just as your bod needs a balanced diet to keep it in tip-top condition, so does your barnet. If your hair is as dry as hay and breaks more easily than peanut brittle, it's probably due to a lack of essential fatty acids which keep it moisturised and supple. These fatty acids can be found in oily fish such as

sardines, salmon, tuna, mackerel and trout. They can also be found in nuts, olives, seeds and avocados. It's recommended that you should try to squeeze in four servings of oily fish a week. Flaxseed and pumpkin seeds are also packed with essential fatty acids – I sprinkle some over my cereal in the morning!

- Drinking around eight glasses of water a day will keep your mane glossy.

- If you suffer from greasy hair, then it may be due to a deficiency of vitamin B. Try to include nuts, seeds, dairy products, wholegrains, green leafy vegetables and eggs in your diet.

- If you've used products in your hair after you've blow-dried it, don't put it up in a ponytail for at least 6 hours. You'll ruin that fab straight style you've just spent ages doing and have nasty old kinks instead!

- Wash your hairbrush once every two weeks, otherwise you'll be brushing clean hair with mucky tools. Our brushes can collect and store a lot of grease and dead skin cells. All you have to do is put your brushes in the sink or a container of some sort, fill with hot water and some shampoo, leave for 20 minutes and then rinse it. This removes all the grub a treat!

- To recondition damaged hair, separate an egg (ask your mum to give you a quick demo), add a teaspoon of olive oil to the yolk and mix. Next, stir a teacup of warm water into the mixture. Massage into your hair and scalp and leave for five minutes. Wash as normal. Do this once or twice a month.

- To sort out Worzel Gummidge tangles, always use a comb and work from the bottom upwards.

- When you are washing your hair in the shower, make sure the water runs clear so that you know that you haven't left any shampoo or conditioner in it. If you do leave any in, your hair will become greasy more quickly and look a bit dull.

- Always brush your hair before you wash it – brushing wet hair can lead to split ends. If you want to detangle wet hair, however, use a comb instead. A comb won't damage your hair as much as a brush might.

- If you get chewing gum in your hair, soak it in full-fat Coca-Cola until it comes loose.

- Always wear a sun hat if you're out in the heat. Not only is this better for your face in the long run (see page 136), but it also prevents the sun from damaging and drying out your lovely locks.

- When those toasty times of summer arrive and you're going to be in the sun all day, then it's really important to protect your hair from the sun, especially if you aren't a hat person. We all know that the harmful UV rays can damage our skin but they can also ruin your lovely locks. They make them brittle, give you split ends and fade the colour dramatically. However, there are products you can get in most chemists that will protect your hair. Leave-in hair conditioners, for example, protect by penetrating the cuticle layer. Read the label so that you know you are getting one that is for when you are out in the sun and need protection – look for one with an SPF formula to protect from UVA and UVB damage.

- There are two reasons for brushing your hair at least twice a day. First, it stops your hair from looking like a bird's nest and, second, it helps prevent all those little dead skin cells that cause dandruff from getting too comfy in your locks.

- Avoid buying hairbrushes made from synthetic bristles and opt for a natural-fibre brush instead. It's a lot kinder to your hair and scalp.

- Wash your hair twice a week if you use styling products. Too many products can dry your hair out.
- If you have red hair and it's looking a little dull, purée eight carrots in a blender (ask an adult to help you). Now bend your head over the sink, massage the mix into your hair, leave for 15 minutes and shampoo. The carrot pigment will boost the red in your hair.
- To perk up blonde locks, rinse them in chilled camomile tea after you shampoo.
- Brush your hair until it's completely knot-free before you wash it. Trying to do so when your hair is wet will only split the ends and cause damage. Only use a clean comb on your hair when it's wet. I always comb my hair through while I'm waiting for my conditioner to do its magic.
- When you're sunbathing on holiday and want a few natural highlights, squeeze lemon juice on to your hair. It's quick, cheap and looks great for blonde or light-brown hair. If done on a regular basis, it can damage and dry your hair out, though!
- If you are hitting the beach and want your mane to look glossy and gorge, not dry and brittle, put a tiny bit of tanning oil into the palm of your hand, rub it around, then stroke it through your hair.

HANDLING YOUR HAIRDRYER

Many years ago, my toe-rag of a pony, Snowflake, helped himself to a chunk of my hair! My dried-out old barnet looked like a yummy little treat of hay just for him, dangling right under his nose while I was busily grooming him. And who can blame him? Anyway, the damage he did was unbelievable – within seconds, my head went from a sought-after delicacy for horses to something that can be best described as a newborn rat!

So the lesson to be learned from this is, don't cook your hair to death with your hairdryer – and, if you do, make sure you stay well away from hungry horses. Here are some more of my tips for working that dryer.

- Before that hairdryer gets anywhere near your locks, don't forget to apply the right product. If you have frizzy or curly hair, a good serum will calm the craziness down; if your hair is damaged or dry, spritz in a leave-in conditioner to nourish the ends. Long locks and flat hair need a mousse wedged into the roots to prevent it from simply flopping down and to give it some lift and volume.

Jodie Prenger – Winner of I'D DO ANYTHING and West-End Theatre Star

Curls are always glamorous but they can be pricey and unhealthy for your hair. Do not fret. There is no need to spend all your pennies on expensive products or heated rollers.

In fact, what you find in your loo does the trick! I don't mean for you to stick your head in the toilet – grab yourself some toilet paper, double it over and then wrap your hair around it. Gently tie it up and spritz on a little hairspray. If you have a pair of old tights to hand, pull them over your hair and this will keep it all in place and it will stop your curls going frizzy. You may look like your great-aunt going to bed but you will wake up looking like a little princess. The curls are fabulous and there is no need to damage your hair with heated products.

- Keep your hairdryer moving at all times. Don't stop in one place to make your hair dry more quickly – the heat will do huge damage and can leave it looking like those frazzled-looking fries that you can buy at the supermarket!

- Don't turn your hairdryer on to full heat. You may as well dry your hair in a clay oven – it'll just become very dry, brittle and will easily snap. So ease up and step away from the hairdryer.

- Point the hairdryer (with the nozzle on) down along your lengths of hair. This will encourage the cuticles to flatten, resulting in hair that reflects lots of light, not like you've just had an electric shock!

- If you've absolutely no idea where to start when using your hairdryer, ask your hairdresser to give you a quick lesson in how to do an easy blow-dry. Check if you have to pay for this first, though. Some hairdressers will give you a quick demo for free, others charge. If they do charge and your mum is paying, then ask her first to see if she minds coughing up for this.

- To help calm down the frizz in your hair, before you step out of the shower, give it a cold rinse.

- If you want a bit more body and volume, then tip your head upside down while drying your hair. It feels a bit weird, but it really works.

- Style the front of your hair before the back so you know it dries just the way you want it. Plus, the front is more important as that's what most people will be looking at when they talk to you, anyway!

- If your hair is looking a bit fluffy poodle once you've dried it, go for a walk in the fresh air. This will help de-frizz it. Alternatively, a bit of hand cream will calm it down.

MAKE-UP MAGIC

So many girls leave the house looking like a drag queen or a Picasso that's gone horribly wrong. Have they heard of mirrors? Make-up brushes do exist to apply foundation and eye shadow – you don't have to use the garden trowel. Of course, no girl would deliberately go out trying to look like her face has spent half a day wedged inside a cement mixer, but it does happen – and far too often. So put down those garden tools, princesses – here's how to become a picture of perfection!

MAKE-UP ESSENTIALS

A Lazy Princess make-up kit should be like a box of her most treasured jewels. Yes, something refined (fits into her handbag easily), well equipped (everything from lippy to lashes) and makes her feel like a million dollars in a jiffy. It should NOT, and I repeat NOT, look like your school's art department has suddenly grown wheels and zoomed out of the building. It's all about having a make-up kit that's minimal but effective and which fast tracks you from beast to belle with no fuss at all. So here's what you need to create the wonderful little bag of tricks that we all dream of.

- 1. Lipgloss – It's the candyfloss of every chick's make-up bag. Go for one that's already in a tube, which you can apply directly on to those lips of yours.
- 2. Concealer – Opt for one that's one shade lighter than your actual skin colour.
- 3. Palette of eye colours – Great for experimenting. If you buy sets with two or three colours in a palette, you can be pretty sure that they were put together because they complement each other and look great shaded together.

- 4. Foundation – Pick a fabulously glowing one that is light in texture and complements your skin.
- 5. Blusher – Little cheekbones add great definition to your face. Choose a pressed powder or a cream.
- 6. Mascara emphasises your eyes and makes lashes look longer. Go for a waterproof variety if you are on holiday or if you're heading anywhere near the water. I myself wear waterproof all the time as I find non-waterproof ones tend to smudge a lot.
- 7. Powder helps to blot out the shine, like blotting paper soaks up grease.
- 8. Brushes for your eye make-up, powder, blusher and eyebrows – these will help reduce the amount of excess oil that you can end up applying to your skin. Choose super-soft brushes so that you don't drag your skin. If possible, avoid buying hard make-up brushes: you can do a test by gently caressing them over the top of your hand.
- 9. A mini bottle of perfume. Rather than lugging around a huge big bottle, I decant some of my favourite perfume into a travel-sized bottle.
- 10. Cotton buds are very handy for cleaning up make-up that's fallen around your eyes. Avoid using them to clean your ears out, though. In doing so, you may end up piercing your eardrums, plus you could be ramming more wax further down your ear. Nice!

GET THAT FRESH-FACED LOOK

I have a special compartment in the fridge where I keep all my make-up (it lasts twice as long) and my face and body moisturisers. That way, when my skin needs a bit of a wake-up, the cream is already chilled and it's a real zingy pick-me-up. Perfect for the morning! Here are some more tips to make your skin look amazing.

- First, never slap your make-up on top of dirty skin – always work from a clean canvas. It will only create a nice little breeding ground for germs and spots otherwise.

- Opt for a colour closest to your natural skin tone. If you don't, you will either have an orange lollipop head stuck on a white body or a white face on a brown body!

- A concealer pencil that matches your skin tone is excellent for covering a zit or any other imperfections, such as scars or dark circles.

- During the hottest months of the year, how about switching your foundation for a lighter, tinted moisturiser? It will look fresher and will look gorge with a tan.

- Take care when removing make-up. Don't scrub away as if you were getting a stain out of the kitchen sink: be gentle!

- Cleansing wipes are fantastic for removing make-up and excess oils, leaving your face clean and smooth. They are great to take on holiday as they come in resealable packs and are so easy to use.

- Mineral-based foundations are fairly new in town, and I'm telling you, if you have skin that's prone to spots, buy them by the truckload! Why are they so good? Well, the powders are totally oil-free which is great news as it stops all that horrid oil from building up on your face, which can cause it to shine like a cricket ball. Mineral foundations (eye shadows, too) are made from natural minerals rather than the usual oils and chemicals so often found in other products. Also, there's another plus side: minerals give your complexion the most amazing glow, almost as if you aren't wearing any make-up at all. Being sweatproof, too, you could even get away with sleeping in the stuff! But I recommend you take it all off anyway before going to bed and sleep with clean and glistening skin instead.

- Before you put on your foundation, cover up any dark eye circles and blemishes with a concealer.

- If you get greasy skin, after you've moisturised your face, stick on a thin layer of primer (a liquid that helps to control the grease and will help your foundation go on smoothly and look fresh for many hours) and then your foundation. This will keep your face shine-free and stop make-up from sliding off your face.

- When buying a foundation, never test it on your hand – this won't give you a clear idea of how it's going to look. Instead, dab a little on to your neck and check it in the mirror in daylight.

- Don't be scared of the staff at the make-up counter. They are there to help you choose the right thing. Plus if you are lucky they might just swing a few little freebie samples your way!

- A dewy sheer foundation that suits your complexion is a great way of evening out the look of your skin tone. It's brilliant if you're going to be photographed at a party or other event!

- If you want a flawless, airbrushed look, a little light dusting of bronzer will do just the job.

- Once your foundation is on and has dried, put a layer of face powder on top to set it.

- Don't go whacking another layer of face powder on top of your existing one as this will start to clog up your pores, which eventually leads to spots. Instead, use mattifying paper to soak up excess grease and shine.

LUSCIOUS LIPPIES

Lips are like gardens. If you don't keep them hydrated, what happens? They dry up and look a real mess. Once they've gone past that stage, you wonder what the point of reviving them is. It's the same with lips. If you don't give them some much-needed TLC then yes, they will start to look like a pair of dried-up old slugs. It's creams and glosses you need!

- If your lips have been shedding flaky skin and look like dried-out puff pastry, I've just the solution for you. Buy a soft toothbrush to use solely for your lips (or recycle an old one). Pop some of your favourite lip balm on the end and gently scrub in a circular motion to remove the dead skin cells. Do this for about a minute then apply another layer of yummy gloss for super-soft lips.
- For dry and cracked lips, put some eye gel under your lip-gloss to fill in the cracks, leaving them soft and sweet.
- A great way to achieve plumper and fuller lips is to use two different shades of lippy. Apply the darker one in the corners and the lighter one to the more fleshy part in the middle of your lips.
- If your lips are all scabby and chapped, the worst thing you could do is to keep licking them – this will dry them out even more. You may be dehydrated so you must drink lots of water. Also, try applying a thick lip balm on an hourly basis.
- A natural sheer gloss that has a nude, yet mirror-like effect is perfect for the party girl.
- For a bigger, plumper pout, put more shiny lipgloss in the middle of your bottom lip.
- If you want to make your own nude lippy, then mix a little dollop of concealer in with a bit of sheer lipgloss! It's so hot!
- A lot of lipsticks can actually be your lips' worst enemy – they really dry them out. If you really want a pair of

full-looking luscious lips, apply a layer of Eight Hour Cream by Elizabeth Arden. It is expensive, but should last for a year and it will do your lips the world of good. You could pair up with your mum and go halves with her.

- Lip stains are less drying than lipsticks.
- For berries and burgundies, line your lips with a lip pencil that's the same colour as your lipstick. This will give a sharp and edgy look. But girlies, PLEASE don't go drawing a massive ugly red line around your lips and then fill in with a nude gloss. It looks so bad and is definitely the No. 1 lip faux pas!
- Double the impact with two-in-one products! If your handbag is small and space is limited, go for a lippy and blusher in one. These sticks can be used on lips and cheeks.

HOW TO ACHIEVE KITTENISH CHEEKBONES

- When you don't have any blusher on you, try gently pinching your cheeks for that rouged look. It will only last a few seconds but at least it's a good solution if first impressions are in need here (i.e. a date!).
- Use a dual blush for cute cheekbones. Start off by applying the darker of the two colours below the cheekbone and then apply the lighter one above the cheekbone. It's a great way to create catwalk cheekbone definition.
- A cream blusher in a fab colour adds a little bit of girly gloss glamour to your apple cheeks.
- Some chicks are blessed with a hot beauty spot, while some of us have to fake them. It's so easy to create a bit of 50s Hollywood style – simply draw it on with a dark brown or black eyebrow pencil. Choose your position (the best place is about 2.5cm away from your top lip on one side of your face) and dot it on.

169

SLUG-LIKE EYEBROWS? JUST SAY NO!

- Your eyebrows are the curtains to your eyes: if they look like big hairy slugs, then they need grooming! Use your toothbrush to shape them – just make sure there isn't any toothpaste left on the brush before you do so!

- If your brows resemble two little dusters, all fluffy and slightly out of control, then, after you've put some moisturiser on your face or hands, smooth your hands over your brows. This will help calm them down – and keep them from looking as if they're having a party on your face.

- Always pluck your brows in daylight. It's far easier than doing so using artificial light.

- Swap slug eyebrows for trim little worms – tweezer away those stray hairs, checking your work every few seconds so you don't overdo it. Only have a plucking session after you've had a hot bath – that way, the hairs will come out with a lot less pain because your pores will already be open.

- As a guideline, draw the 'arch' shape that you would like on to your brows with an eyebrow pencil slightly darker than your natural colour. Check out glossy magazines to see how the models and celebs have theirs. Remember, they should be thicker in the middle and thinner towards the outer edges. Carefully, pluck around the shape with tweezers.

- If you want the hairs to stand up a bit more so you have a better chance of plucking them away, avoid putting face cream on them. Instead, wash them with soap, scruff up and leave to dry, then pluck.

- After plucking, pop a little bit of witch hazel on your brows to stop them from throbbing too much and to prevent infection too.

- If you've got really light hair, there's nothing worse than looking as if you have two big dark slugs slapped to your forehead. Fill in the areas that need highlighting with an eyebrow pencil for great brows with definition.

- Always pluck from underneath, never from above. And never pluck in the opposite direction to the one in which the hair grows. Not only will this feel more painful, if you pluck in the direction of growth, it will grow back flat.

- To achieve the perfect arch, spray a little hairspray on to your fingers and quickly apply to your brows. Brush them into shape using a dry toothbrush and leave to set before you pluck.

- If you have over-plucked, then stop plucking immediately. Luckily, brows grow back pretty quickly, so it's not a permanent problem.

- If your eyebrows are starting to look like two little hairy weasels stuck to your face and you want to keep the little blighters under control but you have no idea where to start, go and see a professional who will shape them while showing you how to do it. Then you can do it yourself the next time.

LOVELY LUSH LASHES

- It's always good to experiment with make-up when you're at home to see what does and doesn't suit you. On a dull, rainy day, check out glossy magazines – they always have really good make-up pictures with step-by-step instructions.

- Once a week, condition your eyelashes with a cotton bud dipped in vitamin E cream or olive oil. This will be a real little treat for them and they will thank you for it by growing more thickly.

- To get those big, but natural-looking Bambi eyes, apply three coats of mascara to the top and one to the bottom lashes.

- When you apply mascara, do a zig-zag action from one side of your eye to the other. That way, you achieve even coverage.
- Always start your make-up routine with your eyes and then, if any eye shadow falls on to your skin, you can simply wipe it away without having to ruin your lovely foundation.
- Try the cheat's way with falsies! They're a bit hard to apply at first, but, once you get used to putting them on, it's well worth the effort. Not only do they add depth and definition but you'll be the focus of everyone's attention because they make your eyes look like massive flying saucers! Perfect if you have small eyes and want them to look larger.
- The general rule is, if you have dramatic eyes then your lippy should be neutral in colour, not so attention grabbing.
- A great way to catch falling eye make-up while you are applying it is to dust some loose powder under your eyes before you start. Any falling eye shadow will drop straight on to the top of your loose powder, making it super-easy to brush away with a big powder brush.
- Towards the end of a mascara's life it can become pretty dry, so to get those last few dregs out, simply pop the bottle in a mug of hot water for two or three minutes to heat up. It will soon become liquid again and ready to apply.
- Baby oil works a treat as a cheap and gentle eye make-up remover.
- If you have little currant eyes and want them to look larger, apply white eyeliner to the bottom rim – this will really brighten and open them up.
- Put your eyeliner in the fridge for a few hours before you want to use it. It will be easier to sharpen and you'll have more control over where it goes. Plus, if you keep your mascara in the fridge too, it will last longer and this will

prevent the germs that live in it from having a party! Store your perfume in the fridge too to extend its life.

- Eyelash curlers will make your eyes look bigger, but curl them before you apply your mascara otherwise you risk pulling your lashes out! You can also heat up your curlers for added effect by blasting them with the hair-dryer for five seconds. Be careful not to burn yourself, though! The metal on the curlers can get quite hot. Just wait a few moments before you use them so they cool down. You might want to get your mum to help out here.

- For cat-like eyes, put more mascara on the outside of the upper eye and apply a light coating on the inside.

- Putting dark colour all over your eyelid actually makes your eyes look smaller than they really are, so blend a lighter shade into the inner corners. This will open up your eyes while giving them a hot, minxy look.

- If you really want to jazz and glam things up at the school disco, then add a dash of sparkly liquid liner as close to your upper and lower eyelashes as possible. For extra impact, add some black liner to the inside of your lower eyelids – it will really make your eye colour stand out a mile.

- Volumising mascara is the way forward if you want flashy lashes – an essential for gorge eyes.

- Once your mascara is on, count to 20 so it has time to dry. Otherwise, if you blink and it hasn't dried properly, you might ruin your lovely eye shadow.

- If you're tired and your eyes look like you have been socked in the face by your little brother, but you really want to hang out with your mates, then it's time to bond with a sheer under-eye concealer. It comes in a cream form. You just dab it on with a clean finger making sure it smoothes in with the rest of your skin colour.

- Also, try to avoid wearing dark make-up in the corners of your eyes – this will make them look heavier and more tired. Instead, pop a little light shadow in the inner corner of your eyes (one that complements your other eye colours). This will really help open them up.
- A light shade of eye shadow makes black mascara-covered lashes stand out more by making them the main focus.
- To encourage your gorge eye shadow to stay where you want it to, apply a thin layer of eyeliner just before. It will act like a base, giving your eye shadow something to cling on to.
- If you're looking to buy some yummy new eye shadows that blend into each other and complement one another, look out for single packs that come with three different, complementary colours. They tend to have one light, one medium and one dark shade, which all work really well together.
- If you're wearing hot orange eye shadow, please don't wear the same colour lippy! It's too much – not a good look!
- I'm not a huge fan of cream shadows – often they go on well, but give them an hour or so and they'll start to slide into the creases of your eye sockets, creating a messy look. Opt for powders all the way, especially if you are in a hot country or out partying.
- Blending brushes are the way forward if you want smoky eyes that gradually go from light to dark.
- Liquid eyeliners give your peepers ultimate definition. However, if you're in a rush then forget applying it for now! You'll only make a mistake, smudge the rest of your eye make-up and have to start again… and then be really late. To stop your hand from wobbling so much when you apply it, rest your elbow on a table and half-close your eye when

putting it on your upper lid. Keep your eyes closed for about 15 seconds once you've applied it so that it doesn't smudge.

- If you're really not confident applying liquid liner, dip a dampened skinny eye brush into a hard eye shadow and apply it in the same way.

- There's nothing quite like getting ready for a night out with the girls or staying at home with them to work out some really cool new make-up looks. Do, however, try to avoid sharing the same make-up tools. Sharing brushes and sponges can cross-contaminate resulting in one or all of you getting eye infections. So ask everyone to bring their own brushes.

- Take advantage of the freebie offers that you get in stores, for example where you can buy three products and get a bag of tester-size goodies for free. You can join forces with a couple of girlfriends, buy one item each and then share out the freebies that you can have fun with later.

'GREASY CHIP PAN' FACE FIXERS

- Always carry 'blotting paper' around in your bag. Like sponges, it will soak up the grease. You can buy this in most make-up departments.

- If desperation sets in and you need to get rid of the grease effect as soon as possible, use a bit of bog roll or even the inside of your T-shirt to soak it up.

- A thin layer of mattifying loose powder is a quick fix for greasy faces. Apply with a large soft brush.

- Although having greasy skin can be a real bore most of the time, you will be glad to hear that there will be benefits in the future for you. The beholders of oily skin tend to age better than those with dry or normal skin, and they tend to end up with fewer wrinkles. Why? Because the oil acts like a deep moisturiser, keeping your skin hydrated and soft.

TREASURE YOUR TOOLS

If you want to look like you've just stepped out of the beauty pages of *Vogue* magazine (and not a hedge backwards), you must take good care of your make-up tools. To look even more diva-like, follow my tips:

- Make-up brushes are like hair: they need washing. So wash them every two weeks with shampoo and conditioner, just like your hair. I wash mine by swishing them around in a little water and shampoo (followed by conditioner) in the palm of my hand in circular movements, gradually working all the make-up out. Rinse, gently squeeze out the excess water and lay on a flat towel to dry overnight.
- Although make-up and brushes go hand in hand, they also like their space when it's time for bed. So, always keep your brushes in a thin make-up bag and the rest of your stuff in a bigger holder. This will help keep your kit clean.
- Make-up hates anywhere hot and sweaty! I keep mine down in the basement of my house, where it's cooler.
- Rather than opening a big bottle of foundation each time

Bruno Tonioli – *STRICTLY COME DANCING Judge*

Girls! Go easy on make-up. Fresh and glowing is always better than tarty.

you want to use it, decant some of it into a little travel-sized bottle and take that around with you instead. Store your foundation away in the fridge. When you need more, just top it up from the big bottle. This will help keep it fresher so it lasts longer.

- Pop your make-up sponges into the end of one foot cut from a pair of old tights. Knot the open end and place in the washing machine (at 30 or 40 degrees) with the rest of your clothes – you can do the same with delicate underwear.

- Make-up, especially compact powder, doesn't travel well. To avoid damage to your favourites, fill a roomy make-up bag with loo roll. This will help secure it so it doesn't tumble about.

GO GORGEOUSLY AU NATUREL

Some chicks view the face as a blank canvas. For them, it's a chance to get creative and express their inner goddess, yet others see make-up as a mask, something they can hide behind. It's a bit like a huge pair of sunnies when you're having a dog-ugly day! But being slap-free needn't be scary, you can still look super-hot and sexy. Here's how to look fresh-faced and fabulous all day long.

- Use a face moisturiser that's non-greasy and oily. Your face will look so much fresher.

- Your posture can kill the look of an outfit or make it come alive. It's the same with your face. If you look happy, then the whole of your face lights up. Look miserable and you'll look older and more tired.

- When you go make-up free, you need to be careful in your choice of clothes and colours. In-your-face brights and blacks will drain all the colour right out of your complexion.

177

Instead, go for neutral colours with some warmth, such as creams, soft greys and browns.

- Just because you aren't wearing any slap, that's no excuse for bushy old eyebrows! Use your trusty old tweezers to remove any stray hairs for a sharper, cleaner look.

- I love to go make-up free because it gives my skin a chance to breathe, especially as I have to wear so much of the stuff when I'm presenting on TV or strutting down the red carpet at a première (it's a hard life!). To successfully pull off the make-up-free look, you must look after your skin, however. To do this, I exfoliate my face gently twice a week with exfoliating gloves. This removes all the dead skin cells to leave it looking silky smooth.

- If you ask boys whether they prefer a lot of slap or just a dusting, the majority will say the latter. They love girls to look like themselves, rather than hiding behind a wall of make-up.

- If you are going for an interview, then remember the golden rule – less is always more. Let the person who is interviewing you see the real you rather than a colourful mask. If your complexion isn't looking too hot, then apply a smooth and natural-looking foundation along with mascara and a bit of sheer lipgloss. Leave the rest behind.

So there you have it, proof that a flawless complexion can be natural perfection.

Erika Hopkinson, age 11, Fairfield Road County Primary School, Manchester

4

Midnight Feasts, Stylish Spas & Successful Sleepovers

FROM DESIGNING THE slickest invitations to effortlessly whipping up a feast of lip-smacking little treats, some chicks are born to entertain... then there's the rest of us! So, if you're stuck for ideas, tired of looking like you've been dragged through a hedge backwards every time you attempt to throw a party or you haven't the foggiest where to start, fear not! Here's how to impress your friends with your party princess hosting skills.

- Firstly, before you organise a party you have to think how you are going to pay for everything. All those treats don't just magically appear out of thin air unfortunately. A good way to raise some dosh is to ask your parents if there are any little odd jobs you can do around the house. Maybe you could offer to babysit for your little brother or do some housework in return for some money.
- Make sure the theme of your party is clear on the invitation. Your buddies won't thank you if they turn up in their PJs, thinking it's a girly sleepover with lots of hot chocolate, marshmallows and pillow fights, only to discover everybody is dressed to the nines in cocktail gear.

- Don't advertise your party on Facebook. You don't want 100 uninvited guests, now, do you?

- If you have a little brother who is a right little toe-rag at the best of times, then make sure your parents remove him from the equation.

- Consider your guests: there's no point in throwing a fluffy pink spa party with Britney blasting in the background if your friends are full-on tomboys, who like to grunge about in jeans and black nail polish, listening to punk music.

- Good parties take time, effort and organisation. On the day before, or even on the morning of the day itself, prepare as much as you can. If you leave it all till the last minute you'll be a stressed-out, grumpy grots when your chums rock up later. It'll also look like you've hired a bunch of left-handed chimpanzees to help out. Believe me, bad news travels fast and you really don't want to hold the crown for being the worst party-thrower ever!

- Whatever your chosen vibe, make sure it's reflected in the way you decorate your party. You wouldn't combine a karaoke machine with a spa evening!

- Imagine you're a guest arriving at your party. What would you like to see and do? Whatever the answers are, do them! This is a great way of making sure your guests feel happy and relaxed and want for nothing.

- Work out a sensible number of people and agree this with your mum and dad. I always work on the idea of how many can dance in a room before the floor caves in and they fall through the bedroom ceiling into the living room, but that's just me! Whatever the number, just take a quarter away and that should be perfect. Don't over-invite. Remember, the more people, the more organisation is needed – plus it will be more pricey because cookies and mocktails don't come cheap.

- If you want to keep costs down, you can always ask your chums to each bring a little something.

- Make sure you invite friends who will whip everyone up into party mode and set the room alight. If you're really rubbish at making things happen, ask your most organised and creative friend over and persuade her to help set it all up.

- Think about the day of the week on which you will throw your party. If it's a weekday, it will need to finish early so you're not too tired for school the next day. Personally, I always like to hold parties at the weekend when there's plenty of time.

- Do you want your friends to have to sit in the bottom of your wardrobe or half in, half out of the room because there's not enough room for them all to sit? Wherever you plan to hold your party, and especially if it's in your bedroom, make sure any clutter is cleared away beforehand and there are places for people to sit. Plus, no one wants to see your dirty socks or homework! If there's too much furniture in there, work out what you need and ask your mum if you can stash the rest in another room, out of sight, for a while.

VINTAGE TEA PARTY

From time to time, every budding princess needs to indulge herself (and her mates) in afternoon tea. There's nothing quite like lying back on elegant furniture, gazing up at the crystal chandeliers (OK, a girl can dream!) and sipping away at exotic teas served in ornate cups and saucers. Delectable pastries and dainty finger sandwiches by the truckload are just added bonuses. Here's how to organise a gorgeous girly get-together.

- First, send handwritten letters to the select few inviting them to your tea party. Remember to include all the details of where and when it will be held. Pop a little pressed flower into each envelope (see box, page 186) so your guests get a feel for the vibe. Make sure you ask them to reply by a certain date so you know who can make it.

- Hunt around charity shops for pretty teacups and saucers. As an alternative to plates, your friends can balance their snacks on napkins. Look for those with a floral pattern to keep the theme going strong.

- To jazz up plain paper plates, lay a doily on them. Then, using acrylic paint and a sponge, dab a pretty colour through the gaps. This will give your plate an ornate lace look!

- You need a waiter – the real thing will be far too expensive, so bribe your little bro to do it instead! Make sure he dresses smartly. No jeans and grotty T-shirts, please!

- If it rains, don't worry – just set the whole thing up in the living room on a picnic rug (choose a pretty one in girly pinks and whites or florals). Create a little walled garden around you and your friends by gathering plants from around the house or the garden and lining them up around the edge of the rug. Check that your mum and dad are OK with this before moving anything.

- Scatter co-ordinating embroidered cushions around the place. Plump them up to make them look cosy.

- Tea-lights in jam jars look divine. Fill the base of each one with sand so they don't topple over and push a tea-light into the sand.

- Serve proper stately-home sarnies – cucumber, egg mayo and watercress, chicken and tomato, tuna and sweetcorn, ham and mustard. Trim the crusts off and cut them into little triangles.

- A good way of keeping the cost down is to buy huge bottles of lemonade or cola instead of little cans – they work out so much cheaper.
- Load up your iPod with lots of fun music or make a CD of all of your friends' fave tunes – ask them in advance. A good little authentic suggestion here is to find some flapper music from the twenties or thirties.
- Dress code here is essential. Ask everyone to come in floral tea dresses (or flapper dresses if their grannies have them in their attics) and pretty pearls. Absolutely no jeans or tracksuits are allowed.

Edible flower garnishes

- **Whole flowers:** Carnation, apple blossom, plum blossom, violet, lavender, lilac, rose, pansy, snapdragon, elderflower.
- **Petals only (remove the stems):** Cornflower, English daisy, sunflower.
- **Poisonous flowers (never use these):** Crocus, foxglove, hyacinth, ivy, tulip, poppy.

Once you have chosen flowers for your garnish, remember they must be washed even if you grew them in your own garden. A lump of mud or a little bug won't go down well with your fellow guests! Pick as late as possible so your flowers won't wilt quite so much. The best place to store them is in the fridge in a mug of water.

- Sprinkle fresh flower petals over mantels, if indoors, and on the grass and rug outside. Fill tiny vases up with pretty foliage and place them in eye-catching places.
- If you want to carry on the floral theme, scatter edible flowers (see box, page 185) over your ice cream, on top of

Press and preserve a smiling flower for an invitation

1 Choose the fresh flowers that you want to press – I get pretty but cheap ones from my local supermarket. Remember, it's not very eco-friendly to pick wild ones. Make sure your flowers are bone-dry (gently pat dry with a kitchen towel), as any moisture on them will make them go mouldy as they dry out.

2 Get an old cereal box and cut the two longer sides free. Put the rest of the box in your recycling bin. Lay a piece of tissue paper (the same size as the two box pieces that you just cut out) on top of them and add your flower. Put another piece of tissue paper on top of the flower, then the other side of the cereal box, thus creating a sandwich effect. Now, find a flat surface, put the flower sandwich on top followed by six to eight large, heavy books. Leave for a few weeks so that your flowers are left to dry out thoroughly and press neatly.

cakes or even over salads for a blooming marvellous look. Flower decoration has recently become a popular trend and it's a great way to add colour and excitement to a dish. But beware: some flowers are highly toxic and can make you feel very sick indeed; also the cut flowers sold in supermarkets have been sprayed with all kinds of insecticides and fungicides and should never be used as a garnish.

- Serve cup cakes galore, jelly, homemade cookies, sticky buns, malt loaf, tiny tarts and English scones with cream and jam. Prepare all the food beforehand and try to persuade your mum to help (you can always offer to do the same when she has her friends round).

- The thing is, you really don't have to spend a lot of dosh for a really cool tea party – two types of sandwiches, a cake and some biscuits plus tea would be inexpensive and still fun. It's getting together that counts.

- Remember, your guests are there to enjoy your company, not see you in your pinny running round like a headless chicken, getting all stressed out. The more you get ready in advance, the more relaxed you will feel.

- Serve a selection of teas – fresh mint tea is a good 'un – it looks good, smells good and is very good for your health. Simply pile lots of fresh mint leaves in a teapot filled with boiling water and leave to infuse for five minutes, then pour into teacups. Offer sugar in case your guests want to sweeten it. You can also make fresh ginger tea. Just cut off a hunk of ginger (peel it) about the size of a grape. Cut into three pieces and pop it into some boiling water. Leave again for about five minutes to infuse, then drink. If you want to sweeten it up, then add some honey.

- Make a goodie bag for each of your friends to take home. This could contain homemade lavender cookies, postcards with your floral design on the front, a mini scented candle, a wedge of cake and a little poem written on really old-fashioned paper in your best handwriting using an ink pen.

THE SPA PARTY

Arm yourself with nail polishes and popcorn, then get ready to pamper, princesses! What could be better than a good old beauty session with the girls? Here's how to create a deluxe night in with all the trimmings – LA style, baby!

- Write and post handmade invitations to the select few, giving details of where and when they will be treated to their heavenly beauty evening at your place. Make sure they RSVP so you know the numbers. Ask them to bring along a pair of PJs and a dressing gown to relax in plus a pair of open-toed sandals or flip-flops so they don't smudge their fresh new pedicures.
- Don't ever use your guests as guinea pigs for carrying out new beauty treatments! Only apply those that are tried and tested. Do little test patches on everyone's wrist beforehand and, if any of the lotions and potions starts to burn or feels a bit uncomfortable, rinse it off at once and don't serve it up as a treatment.
- Create a salon-like atmosphere with chilled music, scented candles (don't leave them unattended), soft pillows and low-level lighting, such as lamps and fairy lights (turn off spotlights and any other bright lighting). Perfect for a professional pampering session, this will help to relax you and your friends.
- Transform your work desk or table into a vanity table and ideally position it by the window for lots of natural light, which is great for doing your make-up. Cover it in a white

sheet or a few large white towels (ask your mum first!). Add some pretty candles, a bowl filled with water and scattered with floating flowerheads, make-up, cleansers, nail-polish remover, powder puffs and mirrors, tweezers, etc. Fill jam jars with cotton wool balls and add a box or two of tissues.

- Warm up your towels by putting them in the airing cupboard or on a heated towel rail. Make sure the room in which the spa treatments will be carried out is warm, too.

- Scatter clean bath towels over your bedroom floor to avoid ruining the carpet with spillages.

- Spray dry towels with your favourite fragrance, place in the tumble dryer for two minutes, then remove and hand them to your guests.

- Ask your mum if you can raid her kitchen cupboards for deep baking trays, big casserole pots or bowls to soak your tootsies in. You could also ask your friends to bring their own bowls and towels to help out so that you don't have such a big post-party washing-up operation on your hands. Each guest needs a pot or a dish for her own treatment. Fill halfway with lukewarm water and pop a little lavender aromatherapy oil into each one (two or three drops will do the job). Take them into your bedroom and line them up parallel to the bed (on which you will all be sitting). Different aromatherapy essential oils have different qualities and different effects. Lavender is a great one if you are hosting a spa party because it helps to relax your guests, helps them to sleep, combats stress and soothes headaches. Lavender oil can come in all sorts of guises – in candles, soaps, lotions, massage oils and bath salts.

- If you're a mani or pedi fanatic, load up on lots of fashion-forward shades of polish (or ask everyone to bring theirs so you have a wider choice and the chance to experiment).

- The best way to organise treatments is to take it in turns. For example, if there are six of you, have three on and three off. Three of you can soak your feet and have the others scrub them for you and then swap around.
- Stock up on weekly gossip magazines (ask your friends to bring theirs too) so those waiting for their treatments to work can while away the time by catching up on what those naughty celebs have been up to.
- I know it creates a lovely cosy environment, but don't go draping a scarf or other piece of fabric over a lamp to dull the glare. You won't score too many brownie points with your parents if you burn the place down!
- Make sure everyone is aware of the ingredients that you plan to use in your treatments so they can avoid anything they know they're allergic to. You won't want anyone going home looking like a giant red radish!

THE TREATMENTS
A little word of warning: sitting with half of the contents of the fridge stuck to your face can make you look utterly ridiculous! But I wouldn't worry because so will everyone else… and that's why I might add that spa days are strictly chicks only. No boys allowed!

Creamy Honey Cleanser
- 1 teaspoon honey
- 1 teaspoon natural yoghurt

With a wooden spoon, combine the honey and yoghurt in a cereal bowl. Using a damp, but warm flannel, apply some of the mixture on to clean, but damp skin. Rub it in with your fingertips, then rinse thoroughly and pat dry with a towel.

Steam Cuisine

Note: this is not for those with sensitive skins! Everyone else, fill a bowl with very hot water, lean your clean face over it and then cover your head with a tea towel. Remember, your face must not come into contact with the water – this is NOT apple bobbing! You are simply allowing the steam to rise and cleanse your face. After ten minutes of soaking and steaming, remove the towel and splash your face with cold running water to close up the pores. Now pat your face dry with a clean towel.

Delicious Skin Scrub

While pottering around in the kitchen, make up some homemade scrub. All the ingredients for this recipe can be found in the cupboard, but be sure to ask first! Get a big bowl and lob a mug of brown sugar (or porridge oats, which are also known as the healing grain) into it. Add roughly ten tablespoons of olive oil. Mix together and take through to the spa area. This is brilliant for scrubbing away at the dead skin on your feet and hands over a big bowl. Gently rub the scrub into your skin for 15 seconds, then rinse with warm water.

Cabbage Mask

This little treatment is so easy and effective when it comes to soothing and healing skin. All you have to do is take two or three whole cabbage leaves and dunk them in boiling-hot water to soften. Once they have cooled off, plonk them on your face. Lie back and relax for about ten minutes, then discard the leaves.

Avocado Mask

This is great for those with dry skin. Avocado will return it to its glowing glory. Mash up a ripe avocado (one per princess) in a bowl. Spoon on to your clean face (avoid the eye area); leave for 15 to 20 minutes to work its magic. Rinse with warm water and then moisturise.

Arguably Appley

Treat your skin to a deep cleansing mask. This will draw all the dirt from your pores and ease the congestion that can cause spots. Grate one apple and combine with five tablespoons of honey per princess; spoon evenly over your clean face. Leave for 10 to 12 minutes. Rinse with cool water and then moisturise.

Satin Strawberry Smoothie

Ask a parent to help you use the blender. Pop 12 extremely ripe strawberries with five heaped tablespoons of cornflour per princess inside. Avoiding the eye area, spoon on to clean skin and leave for 15 minutes. Rinse and moisturise.

Marvellous Mask

For a brilliant DIY facial scrub at home, mix two tablespoons each of sugar and lemon juice together and massage GENTLY over your skin for a minute or two. Exfoliate away until you look like a gleaming goddess.

Teabag Treatment

Once you've finished your tea, don't go lobbing out the used teabags! They're very handy for de-puffing tired eyes. Instead, pop them into the fridge to chill and then, once they're cold, close your eyes and place on top. Leave for ten minutes, then discard.

Tea Toner

This one can be made up in advance and it's particularly good if you live in the city, where your skin can get quite dirty. It will cut down on the grease and grime which cause spots. Mix

2½ tablespoons of peppermint infusion (mint tea leaves that have been soaked in water for half an hour beforehand) with 2½ tablespoons of green tea together and pour into a pretty labelled bottle. Dab the mixture on to a cotton wool pad and gently rub over your clean and cleansed face to remove any dirt. Moisturise as normal.

Hannah's Hand Scrub

Mix together two teaspoons of olive oil, two teaspoons of lemon juice and one tablespoon of granulated sugar in a bowl. Scrub into damp hands for roughly 15 seconds, then rinse and finally apply hand cream to lock in all the moisture and goodness. For a star-quality manicure before you moisturise, follow my instructions on pages 142–43.

Foot Massage

First things first, before you do any treatment that prevents you from walking around for 15 to 20 minutes, make sure you have a clean, dry towel, your mocktail (see below and also page 18) or herbal tea and, most importantly, some healthy munchies. Pop some relaxing music on, light some candles, and fill up your bowls, baking trays or casserole pots with some hot water (not too much or it will overflow when you put your feet in!). Squeeze the magic ingredient (scented bath oil, or a splash of some sweet-smelling bath or shower gel) into the water. Now sit on the side of the bed, pop your tootsies in the water and soak for just 15 minutes (any longer and your feet may end up looking like shrivelled-up prunes!). This will soften and relax them. Take them out and pat dry on your towel. Have a fellow therapist massage your feet with some peppermint aromatherapy oil, or oily body cream for a relaxing and reviving tootsie treatment. Make sure she works the mixture right into

The perfect princess pedicure

1 First, use cotton wool balls to remove all old nail varnish.

2 File the nails in a square or round shape – whatever your fellow beautician wants! But don't use metal files because they can rip your nails. Instead, use an emery board.

3 Fill a bowl about a third of the way up with warm water. Now add ½ cup of milk and leave to soak for ten minutes. This will soften any hard skin.

4 Now remove your feet from the water and work my scrub (see page 191) into your feet for a few minutes to exfoliate until they feel smoother than a baby's bum.

5 Rinse and dry your feet. Rub your fave moisturiser into them. Separate your toes with strips of cotton wool so that, when they're painted, there's less chance of them rubbing together, removing the wet paint and ruining the overall look.

6 Using toilet roll and nail-polish remover, remove the cream and any other oils from your nails only. Apply a thin clear base coat starting from the middle and then out to the sides. (A clear base coat will stop any

coloured nail varnishes from discolouring your nails and is a good foundation for nail varnishes to go on top of). Do not paint on to the cuticles (the fleshy part where your nail meets your skin) as this will dry them out. If you get nail polish on your skin, then dip a cotton wool bud in your nail polish remover to get rid of the mistake.

7 Now thinly apply your colour and then another thin layer of top coat (only ever do thin coats – thick coats won't dry properly and result in a messy finish).

8 Leave your nails to dry for at least 20 minutes before you put your shoes back on.

your toes and the dry bits around your ankles. Alternatively, you could fill up a tub with some warm water and two drops of peppermint aromatherapy oil and leave your feet to soak your aches and pains away for ten minutes.

Tooty Fruity Cubes
Pampering can be thirsty work, so make sure everyone keeps topped up with lots of water. To jazz it up, add some strawberry ice cubes. Make these in advance. All you have to do is put half a strawberry into each of your ice-cube tray compartments, fill with water, freeze and then serve with water. Alternatively, freeze whole strawberries in a freezer bag and pop one into each glass. You could use many other fruits too, such as blackberries, blueberries or gooseberries.

Mocktails

Mocktails are a must at any spa party – *all* parties, come to think of it! Make yours different. Supply all the ingredients (fruit juices, fruits to blend, ice cream, chocolate, mint, ice cubes, milk, yoghurt, cream, etc.) and ask each of your guests to design a drink with the ingredients that best describe them. Now get them to name it! Have plenty of cocktail sticks, cherries and cheeky little umbrellas to use as garnishes.

HEALTHY SPA SNACKS

Beauty's not just about feeling gorge on the outside, the inside of your body counts too. So, serve a delicious mix of food to leave everyone feeling cleansed and detoxed – lots of fresh fruit blended with ice is always a winner! Be careful what you choose. Anything that's tricky to pick up with your fingers may just smudge your freshly painted nails so serve up easy treats that can be picked up with cocktail sticks. Little squares of cheese, mini sandwiches, apple and banana chunks, celery dipped in hummus, olives and tofu are all healthy choices. Here are some more ideas:

- Green tea stops you from feeling sluggish and will hydrate and cleanse your digestive system so you look beautiful.
- Peppermint tea also hydrates a thirsty body and is good for your digestion.
- Homemade fruit smoothies are vital for a glowing complexion. Blend your fave fruits together for a filling and excellent source of fibre, vitamins and minerals.
- Grapes take sugar cravings away, plus they are an excellent cleanser and will help with constipation.
- Nuts are packed full of vitamins and minerals, plus they give you lots of energy. But watch out, they might be yummy and

packed with goodness, but they are also packed full of calories and can be very fattening if eaten in large quantities.

MIDNIGHT FEASTS AND SLEEPOVERS

There's only one way to be crowned the Duvet Diva and that's to throw the best midnight feast or sleepover! Beauty boosters (see above), pillow fights, spicy gossip about boys and clothes, plus tasty snacks are essential ingredients. So, invite your best friends round, heap up the duvets on the floor and warm up the hot chocolate and marshmallows! Here's all you need to know…

- Invitations can be pricey, so get creative and make your own. Use playing cards or those free postcards that you can pick up in some cafés. Write the details on sticky labels then add to the back of your chosen medium and post. This fun idea will make your invitations stand out a mile from everyone else's, plus it gives your guests a taste of the fun ahead.

- Ask if any of your friends has a karaoke machine and get them to bring it over so you can belt out a few little numbers. You never know, there might just be a mini Leona Lewis in among you! Clear an area for a dancefloor as dance routines are a must – I'm talking Rihanna and The Saturdays here!

- Ask if you can move the TV into your room and have a selection of chick flicks lined up. Choose carefully. Boring or slow movies will make you want to sleep, while scary ones will keep you awake all night! A DVD featuring your latest crush is an essential because then you can gossip about how you're going to be his future girlfriend, of course!

- Line all the mattresses up on the floor to make a huge bed so that you can chat away. Or fill the floor with lots of duvets and pillows.

- A few hours before the girls rock up, decorate your room. Put pillows everywhere and place little bowls of scrummy cinema-style snacks (popcorn and sweeties) around the place. The more you do the day before, the more relaxed you will feel – and that's the whole point, surely?

- One rule – any secrets revealed at the party must not be shared with anyone else outside – that's the law of sleepovers!

- Falling asleep is a no-no for two reasons: first, you'll miss out on crucial gossip and, second, you might just wake up the next day with a moustache and a few extra eyebrows stuck to your face if your friends get a little creative and use your mug as an art pad!

- Try not to do the gossiping snugly tucked up in bed. All you'll want to do is snooze your head off! Instead, lie on top of your bed or huddle together on one.

- Persuade your mum to serve hotdogs or taco chips with salsa when everyone arrives.

- Milkshakes and mocktails (see page 18) – shaken and not stirred, James Bond style will also be popular.

- Leave all juicy gossiping till it's really late. Make your bedroom soundproof. Roll up bath towels into long sausages. You don't want your little brother overhearing and then spreading it round your school or, even worse, on Facebook, Myspace and Bebo.

- Write love letters on really cute paper addressed to your secret crush. Make sure you fake your handwriting so he doesn't know who you are, then pop them in the post the next day!

- It's much more fun having an illegal midnight feast! Just make sure you wait until everyone else is asleep. Before the night, check the doors have been well oiled so they don't squeak and work out which floorboards creak – especially any outside your parents' bedroom!

- If your mum and dad show no sign of going to bed, then go round the house and forward all the clocks. Hopefully this will encourage them to retire because they think it's late. Naughty!

- Pillow fights and truth or dare are totally essential!

- The next day, make sure you tidy up any mess you've made. You don't want to risk being grounded, especially if there's a hottie on the horizon!

- Don't forget to organise a scrummy breakfast – load up on sweet pancakes, pastries, hot chocolate, waffles with maple syrup, fruit salad, healthy muesli, etc. Yum!

- If you are hosting a weekday sleepover then it's probably best to set a time that everyone goes to bed. Your parents may have to get up really early for work the next day and probably won't appreciate being woken up with giggles and gossip – this could jeopardise your chances of being allowed another sleepover. At the weekends, I think it's perfectly acceptable to end the party when everyone just flakes out asleep! Just don't be too noisy.

HAVING A DINNER PARTY – THE CHEAT'S WAY

If there's a cheeky little shortcut to creating fab food without all the faff, then, boy, do I go down that road! Let's be honest, hosting a dinner party for your pals can be stressful at the best of times, especially if you are a busy chick. So, why on earth would you want to sweat it out in the kitchen when you can order in a sneaky takeaway straight to your beautifully laid table? So, calm your nerves, cheat the cooking and whip up a storm without any hassle! How naughty are we?

- Order a takeaway so it arrives half an hour before your guests do. Keep the food warm in a pre-heated oven along with the plates. Throw all evidence of a takeaway in the bin!

- If you have bought ready-made meals in microwaveable packs, then take everything out of the packets, put it all into your ovenware dishes and hide all of the packaging in the bottom of the bin. Cook it in the oven at the temperature recommended on the back of the packet.

- To give the illusion that you have been a busy little bee slaving away in the kitchen all day, sprinkle a little flour around the place, leave a few crumbs here and there and stir fry some garlic and onions (even if you don't use them at your dinner party). It will make the place smell delish and it will totally convince your fellow guests that you have been hard at work, even if you haven't!

- Put your guests off the trail of suspicion – sprinkle a few of your own bits and bobs over the cheat food, like spring onion, chives, a fresh mix of herbs or a dash of olive oil. If you are doing a sneaky pizza takeaway, then sprinkle some of your own grated cheese over and some fresh chopped tomatoes.

- In the cake department, if it's a ready-made job, make it look like your own. Dust some icing sugar over cakes, crumble chocolate over gateaux and fresh strawberries and cream over meringues! Who will ever know?

PERFECT PICNICS

On sunny days, eating outdoors can be an amazing experience, but there's nothing more gutting than spending hours preparing and planning a picnic only to have your bag handles break under the weight of all the pork pies and tomato ketchup you've packed! Even worse when you discover on arrival that you've forgotten not only the can opener and bottle opener for your tuna and ginger beer but also the rug to park your bum cheeks on! So, here's your checklist.

- First, work out how many people you want to invite and the venue (by the sea, in the garden, your local park perhaps).
- Make a list of everything you need – picnic food, hamper or strong bag (such as a rucksack), cool bag, hand wipes, drinks, rug, cutlery, napkins, tablecloth, plastic glasses, plastic plates, bowls, insect repellent and lots of sun cream. Tick everything off.
- Plastic cutlery is a must, but if you want to make things a little easier for everyone, bring finger foods such as mini pork pies, sandwiches, sausages, hummus and pitta bread, bananas, apple slices, nuts, raisins, little cakes and cookies are all good choices, as are breads and dips, plus a quiche or two.
- Always take a bin liner to put your rubbish in afterwards so you can dispose of it responsibly. Remember to recycle, too!
- A rug creates a comfy seat, plus it makes a focal point for everyone. Oh, and it helps to keep cheeky little ants away from the food for a bit!
- Old supermarket bags are a no-no – they will only break en route.
- Ask your mum if you can put the drinks into the freezer a few hours in advance until they're rock solid. Having said that, don't put fizzy drinks into the freezer as they sometimes can swell up and explode. Juices, milkshakes and water are all fine. Pop them into the hamper and by the time you reach your destination, they will have thawed out to the perfect icy-cold temperature.

- Take a small umbrella to shade your food – just lay it on its side on the ground and wedge everything underneath.
- If you plan to take a fresh crisp salad, then don't dress it beforehand – it will just go soggy. Package the dressing separately in a mini travel bottle so you can toss the salad in it when you get there.
- Salt, pepper, tomato ketchup, relishes, pickles and dips will all liven things up.
- Lime juice sprinkled over cut fruit will stop it turning brown and keep it fresh.
- Store sandwiches in resealable sandwich bags so they don't fall apart.
- If you want to split the cost a bit so that it's not just you forking out for all of the grub and drinks, then ask your friends to all bring different bits and bobs to eat and drink.

VINTAGE PICNIC

If you want to do a picnic with a twist, then organise a themed one. A vintage 50s-style feast will go down a treat with your friends!

- Ask everyone to come suitably dressed; a pretty frock or shorts – the kind of gear you can imagine skipping off into the fields to go apple picking in. It has to be cute!
- Wear red lippie, long hair in a bun or try a headband and add a little blush to your cheeks.
- Ditch the rucksack for a real wicker picnic basket with lots of charm to carry your goodies.
- Fill up a flask with some proper English tea! Cath Kidston has really cool floral patterned flasks that are just divine and perfect for a vintage picnic.
- Make some homemade lemonade.

- Take a little picnic blanket and floral paper plates and napkins.
- Keep the food dainty. Milkshakes, mini crustless sandwiches (tuna and cucumber, smoked salmon and cucumber, coronation chicken, prawn mayo, egg and cress, roast beef and horseradish, grilled vegetables, sweetcorn and hummus are all yummy options), scrumptious cakes (scones with jam and cream, fondant fancies, bakewell tarts, old-fashioned fruit cakes, raisin rock cakes, chocolate brownies, etc.) and cheese straws.

Jasmyn Rama, age 14, Sutton Coldfield Grammar School for Girls, Sutton Coldfield

5

Fab Friendships

A BEST MATE is like a big bag of salty fish and chips. I mean, imagine cruising into your local fish and chip shop and ordering a fillet of fish without the chips. It just doesn't work, does it? It's like Ant presenting on TV without Dec – something's missing.

In fact, I think friendships are also very similar to the contents of your fridge. Too much of one thing can either leave you feeling a bit bored or happily feasted up and content, while a lack of something else means you feel starved and there's always the possibility of getting a sudden attack of the munchies. The healthiest diet is a balanced one, where there are equal amounts of everything. So here's how to make sure that today's friendship isn't thrown out like yesterday's fish and chip wrapper.

SO, WHAT'S A BEST MATE?

Basically, it's someone who will drop whatever they're doing to be by your side when you need them, even if it means missing the omnibus of their favourite soap. A good girly gossip comes before everything else! Here are some other ways to tell.

- She's someone who only ever speaks well of you and she'll never talk about you behind your back.
- A girl who guards your shared secrets like a hungry dog with its bone – she's super-loyal and trustworthy.
- Someone who puts in a good word for you with that guy you've always had a crush on, rather than stealing him for herself.
- This girl will include you in everything.
- She won't diss you when you're in love, but supports you and is mega-happy for you.
- When you're feeling rock bottom, this chick is the only one who can truly put a smile back on your face.
- She always remembers your birthday and makes a fuss of you.
- She'll compliment you on your hair or clothes; generally make you feel good about yourself.
- She sticks to the plans that you've made and won't bail out on you, even if Zac Efron just asked her out on a date!
- You can't imagine life without her. It's the fish and chips scenario!
- She's someone who treats you the way you treat them.
- Finally, she's honest with you at all times. That means everything from telling you that you have bad BO (everybody is talking about it) and breaking it to you gently that the boy you've fancied forever isn't interested in you.

All friendships should be like that, but perhaps there's someone you should drop from your life? Here's how to decide.

- Perhaps they can't keep schtum about a top secret told to them in confidence and now they're blabbing it round the whole universe?

- Maybe they don't invite you out with their gang of friends or involve you in fun activities?
- Or they're two-faced and saying one thing to you and another to everybody else?
- If something better comes up, they let you down.
- Definitely ditch her if she snogs the guy you've fancied for ages!
- She won't help you sort a tricky situation when you ask for help.
- Maybe she puts her boyfriend before you all the time.
- You don't feel relaxed around her.
- If she starts dating the boy who has just dumped you, drop her now! No matter how much you like him, never put a boy before your best friend.
- Maybe she just doesn't seem to care about you.
- True friends will always smell a rat, so think carefully if your other mates find it strange that you're buddies in the first place!

HOW TO PATCH THINGS UP

Relationships are a little like making a risotto (and not just fish and chips!). They're hard work and tricky at times, but if you put in bundles of TLC, time and effort then it's so worth it and you'll reap the rewards.

With a risotto, sometimes things go wrong simply because you read the recipe incorrectly. But rather than throwing it out and lobbing the burned pots and pans in the bin, it might be worth trying to rescue what you had. If everything really is burned to a cinder, maybe it's time to move on, but, if you don't try, you'll never know. Friendships are also worth investing some time and attention in. Here's how to patch things up with a friend.

- Take her out for a yummy milkshake so that you're both on neutral territory and you can have a good old giggle about how silly you've been. A huge hug is an absolute must and is always an icebreaker.
- Cruise round to her house armed with her favourite ice cream and a really good DVD, one that'll make you both laugh your heads off in hysterics.
- Send her a really sweet text to tell her how much you cherish your relationship and how you love her like a true sister.
- Offer her that top that you know she really loved and always wanted to borrow.
- Listen to what she needs to say to get it all off her chest.
- Sometimes a good old cry together is the best remedy for built-up tension.
- Go for a shopping session and pamper yourselves.
- Organise a little surprise picnic in the park or even in your back garden with lots of homemade cookies, sarnies and lemonade.
- Burn all her fave songs on to a CD to give to her, complete with a really sweet front cover design that includes a photo of the two of you.
- Bake her a cake with all of her favourite toppings.
- If you're in the wrong, don't be stubborn and not phone her. It takes guts to admit you've made a mistake. If you stand up and say you're sorry, you'll earn serious brownie points. So, swallow that pride because life's too short. Get dialling now! If she puts the phone down on you, write her a lovely letter to apologise, then the ball is in her court. And if that still doesn't work, then you know what? You know you tried your hardest to patch things up and now you can rest peacefully.

- Get a pretty glass bottle with a cork lid and pour in some gorge bubble bath. Make a label, stick it on the side and tie a sweet little bow on top. She'll love this, and she can then go and have a lovely long bath and soak away all the stress.
- If you're the one saying sorry and you are completely cacking yourself about delivering the apology, then practise at home (in front of the mirror or to your teddy).
- When you apologise, don't look down at your feet, instead keep eye contact.
- Try to keep a lid on your temper. By raising your voice you will look weak and your friend will want to just back away, which means the whole conversation (or apology) will be pretty pointless.
- If you keep falling out on a regular basis and you're unable to work things out, ask yourself if it's worth pursuing this particular friendship.
- If something's niggling you and it's not that important, rather than nit picking over it, bite your tongue and let the whole thing blow over to save yourself an argument.

LITTLE THINGS COUNT WHEN YOU'RE REALLY DOWN IN THE DUMPS

Lots of people sometimes wake up on a sunny morning but only see dark miserable clouds when they look out through the curtain. Their day is completely taken over by negative thoughts, grumbles and grouches. If this is you or your best friend, here are some strategies to blow away those dark clouds, cheer each other up and let the sunshine back into both your lives again.

- Be creative and do something such as baking a cake, stencilling your bedroom walls, painting a picture to take your mind off being down in the dumps. It will give you the satisfaction of doing something rewarding.

- Dance – crank up your music as loud as possible and dance your socks off. It doesn't matter if you have two left feet and dance like a chimp – don't let that put you off, just go for it!
- Try doing a spot of karaoke in your living room and singing at the top of your voice. You might want to close your curtains, though, so your neighbours don't catch a glimpse of your terrible Michael Jackson moves!
- Treat yourself to that dress you've wanted for ages and that you've been saving up for.
- Clean your parents' car, thus pocketing yourself a nice little fiver and spend it on some seriously cool new make-up.
- Whizz up some fun new recipes in the kitchen and make loads of mess! You might want to quickly clean it all up afterwards, though – unless you want to get told off!
- Go for a long bike ride. Exercise helps to blow away the cobwebs and puts you in a better mood.
- Speed-dial your best chum to come over and watch a good old film over a tub of Ben & Jerry's.
- Make a list of what you love about yourself, and then, when you are having a pants moment, whip it out, read it and remind yourself why you're a good person and have nothing to worry about.
- People watching can be so entertaining! So, head for your local café armed with a stack of your fave gossip mags and order the biggest hot chocolate ever. Watch the world go by as you sneakily peek at it through undercover Nicole Richie jumbo-sized sunnies!
- Do a little DIY gardening – but in your bedroom. I used to grow lavender in one of those boxes that clip on to the windowsill. It's fun watching it grow and it also smells

delicious. Don't stop there, though. You can grow all kinds of plants in a window box, from flowers to herbs to little tomatoes. Your mum and dad can help get you started.

- I also had a tomato plant in the conservatory. Again, it was so much fun watching it flower, then grow fruits and end up in a yummy salad!
- Do something really nice for someone else. When they thank you with a smile, you'll feel really good about yourself.
- Your old clobber could help combat poverty! Have a wardrobe detox and take all the bits that you know you're not going to wear down to your local charity shop. The buzz of doing something good is amazing. Just do it! Remember a cluttered room is a cluttered brain, so having a clear out sesh is very healing and calming for the brain.
- Put on your fave funniest DVD, the one that makes you laugh uncontrollably.
- Positive thoughts will help to superglue a whopping great smile on your face in no time.

MAKING NEW BUDDIES

- Want to widen your circle? A great place to start is to think about what interests you and to join a class or group relating to that. Whether it's dance, singing or sports (or even origami!), you'll meet like-minded people. At least you know you'll have one thing in common.
- If you do decide to join a class, make sure you enter the room with a big friendly smile on your face. Looking like an old misery chops won't encourage people to come up and talk to you!
- Joining a club of some sort is a great way of forcing yourself into a social setting, especially if you are a naturally shy person and find it hard to make friends. Being part of a club

means you have to interact with people in order to take part in things. You see, the more you go, the more you are likely to break down your barriers and start talking to new faces, and before you know it you will probably be making arrangements to hook up with them outside of club times.

YOUR BEST FRIEND FUTURE BOX
I first made one of these with my best bud when I was eight years old. I completely forgot all about it until one day last year when my mum stumbled across it in the attic. Well, we were so excited! We sat down at the kitchen table, dusted it off and opened up the box of the 'unknown'.

It was kind of bizarre, really – a bit like opening Pandora's Box. I felt excited and nervous because, although I remembered

Make a Future Box

Here's what you need:
- A box or a trunk that you can seal up and make airtight
- Velvet or a few old soft flannels

Now write a letter with your predictions and how you felt on the day of making the box. Include your fave CD – you'll be amazed how music changes! Pop it inside and of course add your most memorable nick-nacks. Write on the outside of the box: 'Keep out – do not open till [give a date that's ten or twenty years away]' – and then go and hide it somewhere!

making it, I couldn't think for the life of me what I had placed inside it. So, we prised it open. Inside lay everything on its little velvet bed in perfect condition, all of my little nick-nacks that meant the world to me when I was eight years old. There were hilarious photos, the front page of a newspaper (so I knew what happened on that day), a cute little teddy with whom I had shared some very memorable moments, my running awards plus a letter my best friend and I had written.

The letter was interesting because I had scribbled down a prediction of what I thought I might be doing in 20 years' time. I had predicted that I would be a vet (one glimpse of blood and I'm well and truly on the floor, passed out cold!), a crazy artist (yep, I'm one of those!), a messy and terrible cook (oh yeah, spot on there) and I would live in America (OK, love it there, but I'm really a London chick!). It felt so amazing to revisit the past, to bring up old special memories and it was also really interesting to see whether my predictions were right or wrong (half and half, really). So why don't you and your best mate do the same? Make it, forget about it and then dig it out many years down the line and surprise yourselves!

So, invest in your friendship like you would a good winter coat – one that is reliable, goes with everything, can be dressed up or down and most importantly one that lasts for ages.

Michelle Sloan, aged 14, Earls High School, Halesowen

6

Festival Fever for Every Diva

THERE ARE TWO ways to do a festival. The first option is that you skip around the countryside looking like you're part of Kate Moss's trendy Wendy posse, dripping in stylish, to-die-for clobber, with messy, but minxy hair and fresh, sparkling skin and make-up. Your tent that is so well equipped that, well quite frankly, you could almost be in the grounds of Buckingham Palace, it's so darn comfortable and cool!

Alternatively, there's the second option. Yep, you're one miserable-looking mud monster, trudging around that mud-filled lake as if it was your home, dragging around your sodden jeans and searching for your other shoe, which somehow got sucked up in a swamp somewhere on your journey back to your tent, which incidentally you can't find anyway because you bought it in the same blue as every other festival-goer in the 4,000-strong crowd. Anyway, because you didn't take the time to look for a good pitch it's shot off somewhere down the other end of the field in a heavy mudslide with the other 2,000 blue tents. Your grubby face resembles the side of a pebbledash bungalow, your armpits are producing more pungent fumes than any power station and your clothes look like they've been invaded by a flea colony and then there's your breath… So, the lesson is: prepare before you party! Don't consider leaving home without first completing this checklist.

FESTIVAL ESSENTIALS

Read this mantra before you do anything, girlies! Festival survival is all about style, getting your creature comforts sorted and looking super-cool. If these three aren't in the bag, forget about any wonderfully spiritual experience underneath the stars! Instead you'll have the weekend from hell with rain-soaked knickers and socks and you'll be trudging around in deep mud, wishing you'd never come in the first place. Do your homework beforehand and check to see what the age limit is for each festival!

Here's what you need to know:

P is for… practise putting your tent up in your garden before you go!

R is for… ring your camping chum to make sure you won't double up on anything and you both know what essentials to bring – this will save precious space in the tent.

E is for… your essential kit – read down below for the kit!

P is for… polite. Don't be lairy and loud, respect your neighbours!

A is for… accessories. These can truly transform an outfit in an instant.

R is for… rain mac. Need I explain?

A is for… Ask your parents and friends if they can lend you anything – the more you borrow, the less money you will have to spend.

T is for… tent and torch. It can get pretty dark out there when you're tent hunting.

I is for... ill-prepared. If you don't pack the right things, you'll have a dreadful time.

O is for... OTT. Make the inside of your tent look like a palace – warm, deluxe and super-cool (read on for your must-know tips).

N is for... No one likes a moaner or a high-maintenance chick, so chill out and don't ruin the experience for everyone else!

Firstly, this might sound obvious but make sure you like the people you're going to share a tent with! Being in a small space with someone you can't bear will totally ruin the whole experience.

- Pack everything in a big rucksack or a suitcase with wheels.
- Take a small plastic travel bottle filled with your favourite perfume, plus a clothes peg! Believe you me, when you walk into those loos you'll see the most scary-looking things, so blocking out the smell is something you'll most definitely want to do. Otherwise it may be death by poo! Spray your clothes peg with perfume or simply dab scent (a lot of it) under your nose and then take that brave step into the stinking portaloo but don't look down, whatever you do.
- Plenty of chewing gum will sweeten your burgered-up breath. Also, pack a couple of bog rolls! You don't want to run short of this very important staple. Face and hand wipes are also invaluable.
- A mobile phone is essential – festivals are huge and you'll definitely get lost and lose your friends. This is the way to reunite everyone.
- Take another spare mobile battery with you so that you're in contact with your friends at all times. At festivals they

will often have tents specifically for charging up your mobiles. They're safe, too.

- Wear a bum bag. OK, I know what you're thinking and, yes, I've previously listed them as a fashion faux pas, but, trust me, you'll be the last one laughing when you're fully equipped with all the essentials for survival (your phone, money, water, gum, loo roll, etc.).
- Take a small foldaway umbrella – you never know when the floodgates will open up. Also, No-Germs – it's an instant hand sanitiser that kills off 99.8% of germs and it doesn't require water to work.
- A couple of those foldaway camping chairs will be perfect when you want to do a spot of star-gazing at night or keep your little butt cheeks dry if it starts to rain, rather than having to sit on the wet ground and ending up with swamp-bottom spots!
- Pack earplugs and an eye mask – sunrise is always earlier when you're outdoors! Also, spare batteries for anything battery operated.
- Carry a disposable camera. Don't take an expensive one that could get nicked.
- Looking sun-kissed is one thing, but frazzled lobster is an entirely different thing altogether. Every three hours slap on high-factor sun-protection cream.
- Don't forget to take a pack of playing cards with you just in case it's chucking it down and you need some tent activities to keep you occupied. You can always ask any cute Mr Hotcakes to join in if he's wandering by!

TENT-TASTIC, OR TOTALLY LOST!

For a few days, your tent will be your sanctuary, so slum it in the richest of style! Gaze out on the starry night skies from a deluxe palace proudly adorned with ribbons, bunting and stencils. This 'no-luxury spared' multiple bedroom, Sultan-style tent equipped with servants' quarters (aka the flimsy front door and boot-dumping area!) and banqueting area (the little plastic table on its last legs) must serve your every need, day and night, just as any princess demands. But a tent isn't just a tent, so here's how to find, buy and enjoy the very best of the best, plus how to make your tent the coolest pad in the field.

- When buying a festival tent, go for something quirky that makes it stand out a mile. You'll know what I mean when you get there and cast your eye over a sea of identical tents. Avoid buying block colours such as blues, reds, greens or yellows and consider stripes, patterns or prints instead.

- If you already have a tent and it's blue, green or red, for example, you can customise it with a homemade flag that you can stick on the end of a broom handle, which may be wedged into the ground beside it. Or get some car spray and a fun stencil (ask your parents if this is OK first) and create a really cool design on to waterproof fabric. Stick the motifs all over your tent so that it looks really different. Remember to choose a paint that won't damage the waterproofing.

- A comfy tent = a good night's sleep = not being a bad mood and a grumpy old grots!

- Luxury, luxury, luxury – that's what this whole camping craze is about! Fill your tent with small homely rugs so that when you get up in the morning you can put your toes straight on to something comfortable, plus they help keep the tent warm and insulated at night. Take a warm, cosy throw to cover your sleeping bag, soft chunky socks, incense sticks, an eye mask and a small hot water bottle just in case it gets really cold.

- If you have no idea how to put your tent up when you get there, do the damsel-in-distress thing. Look troubled and confused, bat your long lashes and, before you know it, hopefully a nice guy will come over to offer his hunky services! Plus, it's a great way to make friends with your new neighbours. Alternatively, practise putting your tent up in the garden before you go.

- Many tents are so complicated that you almost need a degree in how to put them up! When buying one, look for one of those Quick-Pitch tents. It will literally pop up into a fully erect tent the second you release the straps.

- Pitch your tent near a landmark. This might be next to a shower unit, a sign of some sort or by an unusual tree, for instance (not beside the loos!). Be aware that these pitches tend to get taken up pretty quickly, so arrive early for first pickings.

- Pitch your tent on high ground in case of floods.

- Before you put your tent up, make sure you lie on your back on the grass. Now see how comfortable that feels. If the ground is uneven, rocky or sloping, you might want to move your tent across a few inches.

- A brilliant way of buying a great tent on a shoestring budget is to scour through the local newspapers and on eBay for second-hand tents. Make sure they have all the components – the poles, loops, etc. anything that holds it up! Without even one of them, your tent is going to look a bit sorry for itself!

- Take an inflatable mattress with you to camp in luxury. See how jealous everyone will be when you rock up with a squidgy bed, along with soft pillow and sleeping bag, and are able to get a lovely night's kip!

- Candles can be an especially dangerous hazard in tents, so leave them at home. Instead, take a large and small torch. The big one can be used when you are back at camp, while the small one is great for night-time missions, such as popping out for a wee or making your way back after you've danced your little cotton socks off and want to return to your tent without tripping on the guy ropes and falling flat on your face.

- It may sound obvious, but don't pitch your tent anywhere near the loos! It may seem a good idea at the time (it comes in rather handy when you need to go for a night-time wee), but, if the heavens open and the ground floods, you might just find yourself with an unexpected guest or two.

- There's also another reason for not parking your tent next to the loos. They get emptied very early in the morning by a huge lorry. It's noisy and the stench is so disgusting – and all of that will waft straight into your tent and up your nose!

- Choose a tent with a little porch so you have somewhere to store soggy shoes and muddy boots.

- Bunting or a bunch of colourful ribbons hung around the top of your tent looks fun and stylish, plus it will make it easier to spot.

- Take a cheap, but funky little radio to blast out your favourite tunes.

- Don't bring anything too expensive with you in case someone decides to raid your tent and nick the lot. Leave the crown jewels and computer at home just this once! You are better off not bringing anything that is valuable or of sentimental value, just in case you either lose it or it gets stolen.

- Take one of those thin, foldaway brollies with you. If it rains, you can huddle underneath it to keep dry.

- If you arrive at the festival and it's already bucketing down cats and dogs, put your bedding in a bin liner to keep it dry while you put up your tent. There's nothing more depressing than a damp and soggy tent.
- Don't put a padlock on your tent. You'll only make it more tempting for a thief as they will think you're hiding something that's worth nicking.
- Take a good-quality waterproof sleeping bag and a pillow that rolls up really easily to minimise the space in your rucksack.
- Get to know your neighbours straight away. They come in very handy if you need someone to guard your tent when you're not there. And then of course you can return the favour and do the same for them.
- Keep your tent tidy at all times, so that when you need to reach over in the middle of the night for your torch you know exactly where to find it.
- Make a 'do not disturb' sign and get it laminated or cover it in varnish so that it's waterproof. When you feel you need forty winks and you don't want to be disturbed, simply hang it on your door and hope it does its job!

Nigel Clarke – *Presenter on CBBC and Nickelodeon*

Be prepared to get mucky – you're not going to the salon! Festivals are all about joining in. And remember, if a jam session kicks off, there are instruments all around you. Believe me, pots and pans can make pretty good drums!

- If you're planning a late one, definitely go back to your tent for a catnap. It will really help recharge your batteries and boost your energy levels.

- A little alarm clock is essential for waking you up for important things, such as not missing your favourite bands. If you do go for a cheeky kip, you'll know you can rely on it to wake you up and get you there. You can of course also use the alarm on your mobile as an option.

- If you don't do any of the above, good luck in finding your sanctuary! It might take you up to four hours of wandering about and don't be alarmed if you walk into a tent or two on the way, only to be greeted by angry faces!

- And finally, it's geeky, I know, but a head torch comes in very handy if your tent takes wings during the night! You'll need both hands to rescue it and fix the problem. Always keep it near your pillow, so if something does go wrong, you know exactly where to grab it to rescue your fly-away tent.

YOUR BEAUTY CHECKLIST

Just because you're going to be living outdoors, under the twinkly stars, for the next few nights doesn't mean you have to morph into the Beast of Bodmin Moor! OK, I'm not saying you should bring a caravan-sized make-up bag to trowel on the colourful stuff as if you were creating a heavily textured acrylic painting or even bring a billboard-size-vanity mirror so you can do the derrière check and practise your Mossy posse pose. Outdoor living is all about being carefree and free spirited, but at the same time it's important not to let your standards slip and to stay fresh-faced and finger-lickin' good at all times. The outdoors will give your cheeks a lovely rosy glow, so take just the following essentials:

- Keep your washbag as small and as efficient as possible. It's all about minimising everything to maximise space in your bag and tent.

- Take a handful of multivitamins with you to keep feeling rock'n'roll.

- Even if you think you won't need it, pack a small first aid kit. If a big old blister starts to brew because your new sandals are on their first outing, then, believe you me, you'll be grateful for those plasters! A packet of stomach settlers could also turn out to be a God-sent gift; also witch hazel for bites and insect repellent – those little mozzies might turn out to be a real pain in the you-know-what!

- Take Deep Heat with you. Because you'll be dancing your little cotton socks off all day and half the night, you may wake up with seriously sore calf muscles the next day. Deep Heat will help take any aches and pains away.

- Pack a travel-size perfume (decant your favourite). Because your body won't be gracing the showers on site (unless you want to come out dirtier than you arrived!), you may just catch a whiff of yourself and it won't be pleasant! Drown out the BO with something sweet-smelling.

- You should also take a mini bottle of sun cream to prevent frying your skin to a frazzle in the sun.

- Batiste dry shampoo is a great camping staple. Forget having to wash and blow-dry your bonce – apply this over your hair to look salon fresh all weekend!

- Cleansing wipes are perfect for your face, armpits, feet and private areas. You'll defo need these, girlies!

- Waterproof mascara – if it rains you don't want to look like a panda, do you?

- Lip balm and lipgloss – to keep lips soft, flake-free and glam at all times.

- Empty some of your favourite moisturiser into a small travel bottle to keep your face fresh and fabulous.
- Last but not least, pack a mini hairbrush, mini toothbrush, travel-size toothpaste and a small deodorant.

SAFETY FIRST

- If anyone offers you a drink or drugs, then say no, thank you and walk away immediately. Never leave your drinks unattended – somebody may slip something nasty into them which can result in you being seriously ill.
- It's totally cool to engage in conversation with people you don't know, but just be aware. There are some baddies out there who may come across as being wonderfully chatty and friendly but they themselves may have other intentions. It could be something dangerous and it could end up messy. If you see them pull out any drugs – you walk away immediately. If they invite you off somewhere dodgy without your friends, say NO. You just never know, and it's so much better to be safe than sorry.
- Tempting as it might be to wander off and leave your friends, especially when you see a really cool stall selling funky bracelets, etc., try to stick together as a group. If, however, you do want to go off for a little mooch, then make sure you tell your friends where you will be and arrange a meet-up time later on. Make sure you all keep your mobiles handy just in case of an emergency.
- No matter how friendly they might be, if a stranger comes up to you and gets all chatty, don't just wander off with them by yourself; take a chum with you. Just be careful!

The Lazy Princess

FESTIVAL FODDER

The thing about being at a festival is that it's junk heaven. Yep, burgers and chips so big they look like logs stacked up against a bungalow, doughnuts that could be mistaken for those rings that you swim with, Chinese noodles in swimming-pool size trays and filled baguettes so huge you could probably sail across the Atlantic in them! Really, it's a minefield out there and your poor old tummy may not thank you for greedily ramming in everything that floats past your nose. What's more, it can be pricey, so choose your chow wisely. You don't want to spend the whole time in the portaloo!

- Ice cubes are a no-no at festivals as they have not always been prepared hygienically and can cause upset stomachs.
- Take a supply of powdered soup sachets with you so that you can make up an instant meal simply by tracking down some boiling water from a friendly person on a drinks stall.
- If a food stall looks dirty, move on to the next one otherwise you might spend more time looking down the loo hole than watching your fave band!
- Keep a supply of nutritious snacks in your tent – nuts, cereal and fruit bars, apples, oranges, canned tuna (with a ring pull so you don't have to take a tin opener, and mini packets of cereal.
- Don't take food that goes off really easily, such as sandwiches, milk, yoghurt, ham, fish, etc.
- Drink bottled water all the time. Don't drink water that has already been opened – it may not be clean.
- Take a couple of soft pillows so you can sit comfortably outside your tent; also a stash of disposable knives, forks and spoons.
- Fridges are a rare thing at any festival so take soft drinks that will still taste OK if they're served warm.

226

- A pack of napkins is great for mopping up spillages in the tent, blowing your nose and cleaning your hands, etc.
- Festival food is always at its best early in the morning. Try not to eat anything after 12pm. It will have been sitting there all day!
- Take a look in the dustbins beside the catering trucks. If they're full of discarded food, avoid eating there!
- Keep a few bottles of water on standby as drinking water and also for rinsing sticky hands. As I mentioned earlier, sometimes hunger can be mistaken for thirst. Instead of reaching for the snacks, try some water instead. If the hunger goes, that's one less thing you have to fork out for!
- If you're going to brave it and try something spicy, have a little peek at where the food is being prepared. If it looks grubby, move on!
- Take a couple of Lucozades with you in case of an energy slump. Handy if you need some help when your favourite band's about to come on and all you can think about is passing out in your lovely comfy tent!
- Pack a handful of bin bags to avoid leaving rubbish around the tent.
- Dancing all day is a great way to exercise and burn up calories, so bring on that ice cream!

FESTIVAL FASHION

It's all about letting your inner goddess out. Yes, I'm talking about Kate Moss-ing and Alexa Chung-ing it up, big time! Festival style means experimenting with new trends to look off-the-scale creative without having tried too hard (even though you might have spent the last four months deciding what to wear!).

- Most of us are guilty of over-packing when we go on holiday, so ditch the habit of taking everything you own to a festival — I guarantee you'll practically live in the same outfit the whole time. It's about being au naturel, with that all-important dusting of glamour. Your festival wardrobe is very similar to the structure of an onion. What? I hear you say. OK, an onion's made up of lots of layers and your approach to festival dressing should be the same. Forget big chunky clothes, they're no good. If it's cold, layer lots of garments on top of each other (which traps in body heat more efficiently) and then, as the temperature goes up, you can gradually remove a layer at a time. So, take a small selection of trendy thin vests, Ts and cardigans that all work together and mix them up.

- Minimise your wardrobe and limit what you take. Change the look of an outfit simply by changing your accessories.

- Take clothing that dries easily so you can simply hang it on the side of your tent to dry later, if you get caught in a downpour.

- Leave the heels at home! Not only will you find yourself locked into the mud like a tent peg but you'll look a total novice.

- Another good idea (just in case it does rain and suddenly 4,000 black brollies take over the sky) is to draw your name or a big flower in waterproof pen on your umbrella. Your friends will be able to spot you immediately and you'll avoid disappearing into the background.

- It's pretty obvious, really, but don't forget your wellies. If you have forgotten to pack them, encourage your dad to turn the car round immediately!

- Fab underwear is always a must for everything you do in life, whether it's going to the gym, shopping or simply leaving the house for a pint of milk. Not only does good underwear make your outwear look better (no VPLs, etc.), it also puts you in a good mood and makes you feel better about yourself. Anyway, even if you end up caked in mud and look all grungy, at least you'll feel great on the inside!

- Don't take your best clothes – they might get ruined. Take your oldies instead. If you want to funk up your old clothes, then give them a mini makeover with fabric paints, buttons, cut jeans into minis, etc. Anything goes, basically.

What to pack

- Really funky wellies to stand out from the crowd!
- Flip-flops
- Sturdy boots or ballet pumps
- Shorts – the better your legs, the shorter you can go!
- Headband and headscarf
- Sunglasses
- A couple of hippy belts will make a plain outfit so cutting-edge
- Selection of necklaces, hippy earrings, hoops and plastic bangles

Scott Henshall – Fashion Designer

Primark (or Primarni!) is a festival godsend. This is when you want fashion to be disposable as, unless you have a Winnebago, you will end up muddy and smelly!

- Floaty dress
- Shawl
- Cardigan
- Kate Moss-style jeans (two pairs – they can take ages to dry if it rains!)
- New and fun underwear
- Rockin' T-shirt
- Plenty of socks
- Denim mini skirt – dress it down with a pair of leggings and trainers
- Plastic bags – if your welly has a hole in the sole or your fashiony-looking shoes aren't waterproof, then wear them around your feet for extra weather protection so they don't become water-logged
- A sun hat
- Keira Knightley-style beanie – a lot of your heat is lost through your head, so, if it's cold at night, this will really keep you warm
- A cool army coat and plastic waterproof mac (one that's light and rolls up, like a cagoule – you can always customise it with waterproof paint)
- PJs, soft chunky socks and cosy hoodie to sleep in
- A disposable camera to capture all those hilarious moments.

BLAGGING IT BACKSTAGE

Being able to see the celebs and band members backstage, but not being able to get near them because of all the fences, barriers and security guards is like being trapped in a cake shop but not being allowed to eat any of them! But where there's a will, there's always a way, girls. You'll probably have just one shot at this, but here are ways to bust your way backstage.

- 1. Wait for a large group of people to file in, all carrying security passes. Mingle with them and pretend to be part of the group. To make this more believable, rummage around in your jacket as if you're about to fish your pass out. If it's a large group and everybody else has a pass, you might just go unnoticed and slide on in.
- 2. Put on your best smile, get some 'good chat' on the ready and head on over to the security man. Sweet talk and flirt with him a little – you never know, he might just let you in as a one-off. Surely it's worth a try? Especially if you just clocked Lily Allen giggling with Kate Moss!
- 3. Befriend one person with a backstage pass. They can then go backstage, get another pass from their friend inside, come out and lend it to you.
- 4. Pretend you work backstage. Walk in, struggling under the weight of a really heavy box, saying it's refreshments for Radiohead and they need them urgently. If you look busy, they may let you fly past them.

FINDING FESTIVAL LOVE

There are so many rockin' things that will make your heart race a zillion miles an hour at a festival, but one thing will give you even more thrills than blagging it backstage and that's love! Yes, romance can bloom in the muddiest places and festivals are brilliant for putting your crush goggles on and meeting the hottie of your dreams as you indulge in your mutual passions of dance, music and muddy fields, so here's how to warm up your flirting mechanism, be a cool boho bunny and score a scorcher!

- If he's looking in your direction and he has sunglasses on and a big smile on his face, you might be on to a winner. Just check you're not standing in front of the stage and he's looking past you at the band!

- So, he's giving you a wink and a come-on sign… First, take a look around you to check there isn't a fitter chick next to you giving him the same signs back. If so, style it out and walk on.
- If he's heading in your direction and you think your armpits might be a bit smelly, keep your arms firmly clenched to your sides like a penguin and don't lift them up at any point. You can always get your mini perfume bottle out and give yourself a quick spritz.
- Having said that, he probably won't notice. Festivals can be one big BO bash!
- Check the coast to see if he's standing next to someone who might be his girlfriend. If he is, but he's still flirting with you, give him a dirty stare and look in the other direction.
- Pop that minty chewing gum in your mouth, fast! If he comes over and smells your beef burger breath, you might just find that he suddenly has somewhere to go… without you!

So, my cool little campers, unless you want to spend three days looking and feeling like one of those minging portable loos, I strongly suggest you plan and prepare every inch of the way.

Katie Sargent, age 13, Range High School, Formby

7

Be An Eco Chick

OK, WHAT'S THE most buzzing trend in the universe right now? Is it Kate Moss's new season's cherry-picked must-haves? Maybe it's oversized, WAG-style sunnies? Actually, it's being seen to be green. Being eco-friendly and transforming your old junk into something new has never been so cool, so get creative and do your bit for the planet. Here's how to do it.

FROM TRASH TO TREASURE

By cutting back and reducing the amount of waste that you lob out on a daily basis, you'll help save acres of land that might otherwise be used for burying rubbish. To get you started, here are some fun and original ideas for wrapping paper using bits and bobs that you may already have lying around the house:

- Fabric scraps sewn together
- Old cookie tins
- Scarves or bandanas
- Newspapers and the pages of glossy magazines

- Posters
- Maps
- Dried flowers can be used to decorate plain paper
- Old sheets of music manuscript
- Junk mail
- Postcards glued on to plain brown paper bags also look cool.
- Tape last year's calendars together for a table covering with a twist or tape cereal boxes together for unusual packaging. Jazz up an old box with paint and glitter, make last year's cards into smaller gift tags and save the bows from presents given to you and recycle them on other gifts.

BE ECO-FABULOUS!

Forget Mount Everest being the world's highest mountain, it will soon be a landfill site that will snatch that crown. The amount of rubbish that we throw out on a daily basis is astonishing. But, you see, as we ram our ever increasingly greedy dustbins full with our clutter and clobber, with not a care in the world as to where it ends up, what we are actually doing is ruining our beautiful planet. So sooner or later it won't be stunning green trees lining our horizons, it will be fermenting rubbish instead. So here's how to be eco fabulous and keep those dustbins on a strict diet!

- Turn old jam jars into jewellery- and hair-bobble storage pots.
- Are scrambled eggs on the menu tonight? Check with mum or dad and, if so, don't throw out the shells or the egg box. Instead turn them into an unusual candleholder! Wash the shells carefully, let them dry on a tea-towel and then pop them back in their cardboard box. Fill each one halfway with candle sand (powdered wax which allows

you to turn almost any non-flammable object into a candle – glass jars are good too). Finally, add a wick to each one – pop it into the middle and sprinkle more candle sand around it.

- You can also use candle sand for refilling candles that have burned down the middle – great if you love a candle and want to get more life out of it!

- Turn old water bottles into homemade instruments. Fill halfway with rice or sand, even small pebbles. Pop the lids back on and shake and groove away! This is a really fun idea for when you're camping and want some natural music kicking off the vibe.

- If you are a bookworm, join a library and borrow books to save money, plus you'll save trees being cut down. You can also borrow DVDs and CDs from the library and even use their computer facilities if needs be.

- If you're off to the shops, don't forget to raid your stash of plastic bags at home rather than picking up new ones. This is a really easy way to save plastic. Alternatively, always carry a little fabric bag, one that easily rolls up into your handbag.

- Don't overfill your bath and, when cleaning your teeth, turn the water off while you brush them and only turn it back on again when you need to rinse.

- Don't leave all the lights on in the house! Only have lights on in the rooms that you're using. Encourage everyone else in your family to do the same. Imagine how much money you will be saving your parents in the long run!

- Rather than turning up the heating a few extra notches because you're cold, put a cosy sweater on instead. Save the universe while looking stylish!

- Thread old buttons together to make a really stylish bracelet.

- Use the sides of a cereal box or a washing powder box to make really cool, retro birthday cards – just cut them out and write on the back of them.

- Recycle whatever you can – glass jars, paper, plastic, cans, newspapers, etc.

- If you're not using your TV or DVD player, turn it off at the mains. Leaving it on standby with the little red light on still uses up energy.

- Give something old a new lease of life – turn an old jam jar into a hurricane candle lamp simply by filling the bottom with sand and popping a little tea-light inside. Transform a baked bean tin into a storage pot for pens, use old cereal boxes as little containers to divide up your underwear drawer (chop the boxes in half first so they're not too tall). The list goes on… It's surprising what you can reuse when you're creative about it.

- If you've given your wardrobe a bit of a detox, rather than lobbing everything into the bin, give old clothes a new lease of life. Sell the good bits on eBay to get extra cash, have a swapping session with a friend, customise if you can or take

Terri Dwyer – *Television Presenter and Actress*

If there's a spare magnetic spice rack kicking around the place at home, then nab it! Fill it up with all of your precious necklaces and earrings, etc., then hang it on the back of your wardrobe door to keep your jewellery safe and to prevent it from being trodden on!

them down to your local charity shop. Your unwanted stuff might be somebody else's new, loved pieces. Also any money raised will go to a good cause.

- When you grab yourself a glass of water, don't run the tap until it turns cold – you'll waste so much precious water, possibly up to 2 litres. Just fill a jug with water and pop it in the fridge. I fill up lots of little Evian bottles and, when I want one, I just grab it (wash the bottles every few days in washing-up liquid to avoid germs).

JUNK MAIL GEMS

How often do you come home and try to open the front door, but are unable to do so because of all the junk mail that's been wedged through the letterbox? Not only does it clutter up the house, but a lot of trees are cut down each year to produce these annoying leaflets. Rather than lobbing them out, use them to make paper! Now, a bit of boring history info here – it was the ancient Egyptians who invented the substance papyrus, which is like the paper we know today. It is believed that it was a mixture of hemp, mulberry bark, rags and water all mashed up into a pulp, then pressed to extract the excess water and hung to dry. Today there is a revival in making the stuff which can be so much fun, plus it's a wonderful way of recycling waste.

Having said that, not every piece of junk mail that lands on your doormat is right for recycling (shiny and glossy surfaced papers, for example). The whole process is really easy and fun to do, and not only will you be helping to save trees, you'll also be making your own unique paper. I use this paper for all sorts of occasions, from writing a thank you letter to wrapping up a present. It may be a good idea to run this recipe past your parents first just to make sure they are happy with you doing it – it can get a bit messy !

The great thing about making paper is it's all about experimenting with different fibres so don't be afraid to think outside the box with unusual things, such as:

- Newspaper
- Egg cartons
- Old cards
- Seeds
- Scraps of yarn
- Dried flowers
- Tinfoil
- Toilet paper (unused please!)
- Magazines
- Paper bags
- Non-waxed boxes
- Computer paper
- Napkins
- Leftover wallpaper pieces

Supplies that you will need:

- Sponge
- Window screening mould – get from an art and craft centre
- Plastic tub or bucket – large enough to immerse your screen
- Food processor for making the pulp
- Flannel fabric
- Staples
- Tacks (for tacking the screen on to the frame)
- Liquid starch

1 Firstly, rip the junk mail or other recycled materials into small pieces and pop into the blender (about half full). Fill the blender with warm water (your paper and water ratio should be 3:1. So the majority being the paper: run the blender slowly at first, then whack it up a few knotches, until the pulp is smooth and well blended (30–40 seconds should be long enough). Check that no flakes of paper remain. If there are, then blend for a little longer. If you want the food to be a different colour, let's say pink, then it's at this point that you add a few drops of pink food colouring.

2 The next step is to make the mould. The mould in this case is made by simply stretching fibreglass screen (plain old door and window screen) over a wooden frame and stapling it. It should be as tight as possible.

3 Fill the basin about halfway with water. Add three blender loads of pulp (the more pulp you add the thicker the finished paper will be). Stir the gooey mixture.

4 Now is the time to add the liquid starch for sizing (this is not necessary but if the paper is going to be used for writing on you should add some. The starch helps to prevent the inks from soaking into the paper fibres). Stir two teaspoons of liquid starch into the pulp. Place the mould into the pulp

and then level it out while it is submerged. Gently wiggle it side to side until the top of the screen looks even.

5 Slowly lift the mould up until it is above the level of the water. Wait until most of the water has drained from the new paper sheet. If the paper is very thick, remove some of the pulp from the tub. If it is too thin, then add more pulp and stir the mixture again.

6 When the mould stops dripping, gently place one edge on the side of the fabric square (flannel). Gently ease the mould down flat, with the paper directly on the fabric. Use a sponge to press out as much water as possible. Wring the excess water from the sponge back into the large plastic tub.

7 Now comes the tricky part. Hold the fabric square flat and slowly lift the edge of the mould. The wet sheet of paper should remain on the fabric. If it sticks to the mould, you may have pulled too fast or not pressed out enough water. It takes a little practice. You can gently press out any bubbles and loose edges at this point.

8 Repeat the steps above, and stack the fabric squares on a cookie sheet. Save one fabric square to place on the top of the stack to cover the last piece

of paper. Use another cookie sheet to press the remaining water out of the stack (do this outside or in the bathtub as it can be messy).

9 After you press the stack, gently separate the sheets. They can be dried by hanging them on a clothesline or laying them out on sheets of newspaper. When they have dried, peel them off the fabric and Voila! You have perfect princess paper!

10 Just a little extra note here – if you find the paper has curled up at the edges when dry, pop a tea-towel over it and iron the edges.

MORE WAYS TO HELP SAVE THE PLANET

- Avoid using the dryer as much as possible. If it's raining outside, hang your clothes on a drying rack, or on hangers and then dangle them off doorknobs.
- Recycled paper is always better than non-recycled, so always check the packaging.
- Carry your packed lunch in reusable storage containers. Studies show that the biggest waste offenders are sandwich bags, foil packaging of convenience foods and plastic water bottles.
- Turn old pillowcases into drawstring bags for your trainers or handbag protectors.
- Transform an old slatted window shutter into a magazine rack. Ask your mum or dad to help you on this one. All you have to do is nail the shutter (so the slats are

horizontal) to the wall with the shutter slats facing upwards so that you can wedge magazines or cds into them.

- Jazz up old files with a slap of leftover paint. Add a lick of clear varnish afterwards so they hold their colour and won't chip.
- Recycle telephone directories, newspapers, photographs or magazine clippings by covering old shoeboxes and files with their pages. It looks really smart if you make them look all the same. For example, cover five different-sized boxes in newspaper, papier-mâché style. All you have to do is rip the newspaper into shreds and lightly coat each piece in wallpaper paste. Lay them on the outside of the boxes (don't forget the lid), overlapping each one to cover. Smooth down with your palms, leave to dry for about six hours or, even better, overnight and give each box a lick of clear varnish to strengthen and keep them in good nick.
- Alternatively, use the same technique to jazz up an old flowerpot or vase, or even the top of a desk that could do with a facelift – very cool!
- Ask your parents if you can personalise a lampshade with Polaroids. Simply cut a few squares here and there from the lampshade with a scalpel (be very careful when using a scalpel and get your dad to help out. Remove the back of the photos and fasten them to the inside of the shade with strong clear tape. When you switch the light on, your photos will be illuminated, a bit like a photographer's light-box.
- Decorate old mirrors and picture frames with ribbons, buttons, gems, stickers, stencils and driftwood.

So you see, it's better to be green these days. The more you can re-evaluate, recycle and reuse, the better. You're not only

being arty and turning your junk into gems, but also saving money because you're reusing the old and creating something new and unique, plus you'll be saving our planet from becoming one big stinky, rotten rubbish dump.

Joe Horne, age 11 Thomas Deacon Academy, Cambridgeshire

8

Frogs, Toads... and Yummy Princes

THERE'S NOTHING LIKE a hot crush to notch up those heart-racing moments and the feel-good factor, but what is it about a good-looking guy that turns otherwise cool, level-headed girlies into slightly obsessed lunatics, who sit close to the phone all day, willing it to ring, or wanting to text him every second on the second?

Crushes have the ability to make us feel wobbly or a bit fuzzy and light-headed. Some say dating is very similar to being trapped in the desert without food or a drop of water. Your eyes trick you into thinking you can see a big tasty Knickerbocker Glory covered in chocolate sprinkles or a thirst-quenching Coca-Cola packed full of ice, only to get to them to find... nothing! Just sand and more sand.

But on the chat front with the chicks... well, it's our favourite topic, right? Talking about all those lovely hotties or horrid toads, dissecting and shredding every snippet about them. My goodness, it's a jungle out there and only the fittest will survive! So, here's how to pick and choose your boys like a box of assorted chocolates... and how to avoid dates from hell.

WHAT BOYS LOVE ABOUT US

- Boys love chicks with their own lives that don't hang around their necks like a scarf. Basically, that means not sitting around waiting for the phone to ring (or at least not letting on!) and instead hanging out with your own friends from time to time, doing cool and fun things.
- Boys love a girl who can eat – they find it dead sexy. OK, you don't need to take on the role of a hungry vacuum cleaner but a girl who likes her grub and enjoys it to the max is so attractive. Boys find it off-putting when a girl pushes and slides her food around the plate.
- Boys love a good hunt. So, don't be easy prey! Make them work hard for your attention. A little chasing will make them appreciate you so much more.
- Always be the first to end a phone conversation even if you're in the swing of some seriously good chat and dying to spend at least another eight hours on the phone to him. Plus, your parents won't want you on the phone all night seeing as they are the ones who have to pay the bill. Tell him you have to dash – you've got to go out (even if you're not going, just pretend). Don't tell him where or who you'll be with, leave him wondering – it will make him keener.
- Guys find it very attractive if a chick receives a compliment happily. If he says you look nice, thank him without going all giggly and shy. This shows you're a strong and confident lady.
- Guys like a girl who feels comfortable in her own skin – basically a chick who is happy, confident and not forever comparing herself to other girls and putting herself down.
- OK, you might be totally blown away by your new hottie, but don't let him know that in the beginning stages. Keep him guessing and you'll keep the tension and challenge alive. He'll love it!

- Don't be predictable. Keep him guessing about where you are on the odd occasion. If he rings, call him back three hours later and tell him you were busy doing something cool. It's not playing games and it will keep him on his tippy toes.

- Get scent-sational and spritz yourself with a sweet-smelling perfume so you're good enough to eat. It's the perfect potion for that first kiss, and I promise it will leave him drooling and wanting more.

- If it's not interesting, don't bother saying it! He doesn't want to know what you bought at the supermarket or if you've tidied your cupboards out. Leave him wondering what you get up to. It's all about being a mysterious little bee, so keep that cool chat just for him.

- Never bitch about other girls to a boy! It'll just come across as sour grapes. If you've got something a bit catty to say, save it for when you're with your best friend, who won't pass judgement.

- It's far cooler not to change plans to accommodate him. He'll respect you so much more as it makes you appear like the strong, independent and confident gal you are, whose life doesn't revolve around boys.

HOW TO PUT HIM OFF

- Trowelling heavy make-up on your face in the hope of getting that airbrushed magazine look can be very unattractive. Boys want to see your natural face enhanced by minxy make-up, not an entire make-up counter stuck to it!

- Make Bridget Jones-style phone calls late at night, telling him how much you love him when you've only been dating for a week. If you are especially prone to this, then write his phone number down at home and delete it from your mobile.

- Talking about your ex a lot is an absolute no-no (he'll assume you're still hung up on him), as is trying to squeeze information out of him about ex-girlfriends.
- Saying 'I love you' before he does. He may not be ready to hear this and it could freak him out.
- Boys hate needy girls who are always fishing for compliments.
- Lettuce-leaf pickers (girls who push their food around the plate rather than eating it) are a real turn-off.
- If you do happen to know what his ex looks like and you also know that he really liked her, whatever you do, don't try and copy her look in any way. He'll see straight through this. Instead be yourself, be confident and relaxed – he'll love you for it!
- There's nothing more sickening than someone who doesn't have an opinion and acts like a little doting puppy, agreeing with everything. If you don't agree or think differently about something, say so. It's so much more attractive and he'll definitely like the challenge. But don't be over-opinionated or you'll do his head in by sounding like a right old misery guts!
- Don't suffocate a boy – let him breathe. Give him lots of space to do his own thing (boys' stuff) and, in the meantime, get on with yours. This will result in him wanting to spend more time with you.
- Constantly asking a guy what he's thinking will eventually start to annoy him.
- Don't babble or giggle like a little girl – boys cringe at the thought.
- Don't nag him to death if he's done something that you

don't agree with. He's big enough to realise he's done wrong, so let him work it out for himself.

- Chicks completely underestimate how important it is to have nice feet. So, if yours look like, or indeed they are, the perfect breeding ground for growing mushrooms, boys will only assume the rest of you is the same. Yuck!

- I'm all for making an effort, but if you try too hard you can actually end up scaring off the boy you like. He'll think of you as high maintenance, and too scared to have fun in case your hair gets ruined or your jacket becomes creased. A boy won't notice if you take one minute (or five hours to get ready) but he'll soon spot someone who doesn't know how to let her hair down and takes herself too seriously, believe you me!

HERE COME THE BOYS

So, where's a good place to meet a potential boyfriend and what do you do once you've got one? Meeting Mr Lush Lips can be terrifying at the best of times. In fact, given the choice of running down the street wearing a fancy dress chicken suit with a big giant toilet seat stuck to your head, or going up to a potential date and saying hello, the first option definitely seems easier! But, you know what? It's never as scary as you might think. The trick is to fake confidence – that's right, head high, take a deep breath and strut on over, smile sweetly and say hello. Now hopefully he won't be able to resist your charms and wonderful sense of humour, but, if he sniggers in your face, here's how to handle it.

- OK, be honest here: have you ever met anyone while you're moping around at home in your PJs? So, motivate yourself to phone a friend, go into town looking gorgeous and start meeting new people.

- If you get a bit nervous talking to strangers and find the whole thing really scary, try this – practise chatting to little old ladies that you don't know. Open doors for them and talk to them about anything (they love a good old gossip!). This will really build up your confidence when it comes to talking to someone your own age. I promise it won't be so scary!

- If you're going to a party and your friend has let you down so you have to go all by yourself, don't miss out on this opportunity. You'll be surprised how many people will come up and talk to you when you're on your own. Be careful, though, and make sure your parents know where you are, what time you're coming home and how you will be getting home. Maybe they will come and collect you.

- Bit embarrassed about heading into a party solo? Just hide behind a bush and wait for a batch of 'dudes' to cruise on up to the door then attach yourself to the end of the group. That way, it will look like you've turned up with the cool crew!

- On entering a party, don't make a beeline for someone you already know. Instead, stop, glance around the room to check out possible fitties to talk to later, then go and chat to your friends.

- There's no point in sitting in the corner at a party because no one will see you and you won't be able to check out the talent! Stand as close as you can to the entrance so you spot anyone coming in – it's always the best place to people watch.

- If your natural expression is one of a miserable old snarly monster, change it! Who's going to approach you if you've a face of thunder on you? Be friendly and put a big smile on your face.

- There's one little phrase that you must ban from your mouth and that is 'He's out of my league'. First, maybe he rates you big time, thinking YOU are way too cool for school, but he'd love to come over and talk to you and, second, maybe you're too good for him?

- When you're introduced to a boy who takes your fancy, make sure you hold his gaze for a moment longer than you normally would. Even if you feel shy, try to wedge a cheeky little smile in there somewhere.

- To ooze confidence, walk into a venue like you own the place and smile, even if you feel quite timid inside and want to hide.

- If you feel really nervous when chatting to a possible date, imagine you're with your best male friend, having a giggle and gossip. This should relax you, so you enjoy being chatted up.

- Being relaxed on a date makes the other person feel comfortable too. The same goes for being nervous – if you look like you're about to freak out, then it's possible your date will pick up on it and do exactly that!

- If you've just split up from a boy and you're still feeling hurt and very vulnerable, maybe now isn't the time to be looking for a new one? You'll only end up becoming needy and might just drive a good one away, leaving you feeling worse. Build yourself back up by learning to love yourself again and being happy to be single. Eventually you will feel confident again. Only then should you get back out there on the dating scene.

- Try to go to places with lots of atmosphere so that, if there are any awkward silences, the music or general banter in the place will fill them, plus it's so much fun people watching together. Having said that, avoid venues where the music is so loud that you can't hear what you're both saying!

- If you are old enough and your parents agree to it, how about getting an evening or Saturday job in a restaurant or café? You'll meet lots of new people and, you never know, you may just find a potential boyfriend.

- Going to an art gallery is a great place for a date if you're a creative type. You'll have something to discuss afterwards over a yummy chocolate smoothie.

- We usually attract people with similar personalities to ourselves, so work on being the type of person that you'd like to meet.

- Being attractive on the inside makes you a lot more attractive on the outside.

- If you see a fittie across the room, stand tall and confident. You'll be irresistible. If you feel unsure about this, practise at home in front of your mirror.

- Feeling too nervous to smile? Just fake it and eventually your smile will turn into a real one!

- If you're at a party and your crush asks you to dance, play it cool. Flutter your eyelashes at him, but don't go over and join him. Make him work for your attention. If he comes over, don't act like a full-on minx by taking his hand and dragging him over to the dancefloor – it's way too keen!

- Fancy a fit surfer boy? Consider getting a summer holiday job as a waitress or ice-cream chick at a seaside resort.

- Shrinking violets who stick to their friends like they're joined at the hips will never get noticed! Act confidently, even if you don't always feel it inside. Having said that, boys find it equally unattractive when a girl is totally loud – believe me, he'll want to run a mile!

- Listen to your date's lingo and try to use a little of it in your conversation. This will make him feel more relaxed and at ease so the conversation flows freely.

- Do let your friends know that you're looking to meet a boy so they can invite you to lots of get-togethers where you might just meet Mr Perfect.

- Gather up some courage and get to know people outside your social circle. This is especially good if you don't fancy anyone in your crowd and it saves embarrassment further down the line if you split up.

- Interesting people attract others, so start up a hobby or two! This could be anything from hip-hop classes to climbing-wall lessons. At least you'll have something in common.

- There's nothing worse than a try-hard – you'll stick out like a sore thumb. So rather than laughing like a hyena on mega-volume at every single joke because you're scared of not fitting into a situation, take a chill pill, be sweet and friendly – and, most importantly, be yourself.

- Ask your friends to set you up with one of their single friends. This could be a disaster (always good fuel for a girly gossip with the chicks when you can just laugh about how bad it was) or maybe it'll be such a success that you end up having a hot boy on your arm. If you are going out on a blind date then just make sure you tell your friends or parents where you will be and what time you will be home. Don't forget to stash your mobile in your handbag just in case of emergencies (one of them being you hate the date and need your friend to do a 'pretend' distressed buddy call, so that you have an excuse to leave immediately!).

- When you see a boy that you quite fancy and you want to get the message across, start twiddling with your hair and give him a cheeky little smile!

- Asking a fittie lots of questions will help you decide whether you're right for each other, plus it's always a good move – he'll love talking about himself! You could ask him anything from what hobbies he likes to what music he's in to, what's the best holiday he's been on, etc.

- If you want to meet a guy just like you, then start doing activities that he would also enjoy, such as walking, joining a book club, etc. You're more likely to be suited because you already have something in common.

- You never know where you might meet your future boyfriend, so always keep an open mind. It could be in the strangest of places, such as the bus stop, at the recycling centre or even waiting for your cake at the deli counter!

- A big smile with a carefree attitude instantly makes you look prettier and more approachable.

- If you've swapped numbers with a boy, don't torture yourself by staring at your mobile, waiting for it to ring. Go out and do something fun with your friends. If he phones, it's a bonus. And if he doesn't... well, what a loser!

SO, WHAT MAKES HIM A GOOD 'UN?

- He makes you laugh your head off
- He wants you to hang out with him and his mates
- He phones when he says he will and doesn't play stupid games
- He puts you before footie (most of the time!)
- He makes you feel super-special and treats you when he can
- He's a good listener and loves to hear about your life – he wants to learn about you
- He organises fun dates
- He's punctual, arrives at places before you and doesn't leave you standing there like a goof!
- He's polite to your parents
- He comes from a nice family where they all love each other
- He loves his mum

HE'S SO NOT WORTH IT...

- If he takes you out with his friends or to a party, but then wanders off as soon as you arrive, leaving you on your own. Either he's not that interested in you or he has no manners at all!
- If you are out on a date and he keeps texting. From my experience, this could be another chick!
- Perhaps he's forever looking over your shoulder at the disco or party? Forget him! He's obviously got wandering eyes!
- Never date a boy who's already going out with a fellow chick. He's bad news and will probably treat you the same – and that spells heartbreak!
- If you are the one always making an effort to organise fun things to do and he can't be bothered, lose him!
- If you're out on a date and he starts chatting up other girls in front of you, then leave pronto!
- If you've sent a text and he hasn't replied at all, then he's just not interested. Don't send him more messages: he's ignoring you! Delete his messages and his number now.
- If your new crush is pushing you past the smooch stage and you don't feel ready or comfortable (maybe you've discussed this with him and he's still not listening), quite frankly you deserve a whole lot better, so send him on his way!
- Communication is key in a relationship. Without it, expect hidden secrets, a broken heart and mixed messages. If there's a problem, get it out in the open and discuss it. This gives you both the chance to see whether you're compatible and whether it can be fixed.
- But if you're really not happy, then don't struggle on thinking any boy is better than none – you're better off on your own and out having fun with your friends.

THE RULES OF FLIRTY TEXTING

- If you're feeling down in the dumps, don't go sending the boy you like sad or emotional messages. He'll delete your number from his phone list and run a million miles! When you're feeling down and need a bit of cheering up, call your friends, not your crush.

- Don't play games, but don't make things too easy for him. He has to work! So, ease up on the texts and play a little bit hard to get because the more you ration him off, the keener he'll be.

- At the very beginning, don't give him too much information each time you text him. Be more mysterious than that. Keep the texts short and sassy, so you leave him wanting more.

- As things are hotting up between you and it's obvious you both like each other, then, if you're on one of those pay-as-you-go schemes, make sure you have enough credit before you start 'to and fro' texting.

Duncan James – Singer

The middle of your school exercise book was meant for love notes, not lesson notes! That's right, if you fancy someone then don't take pages from the back of the book, otherwise you will get caught out. Simply write your note on to the paper from the middle of the book and ask whoever it is you fancy to tick one of two boxes – yes or no, would they like to go to the cinema with you later? This is a really fun way of asking somebody on a date and less embarrassing than doing it face to face!

- Once you've written your cheeky message, make sure you send it to the right person. Your little brother or auntie might be slightly embarrassed!
- Rein it in! Ration him to just one little kiss on the end of the message, not a whole page.
- If you want him to reply to you, send him a text with a question in it.

WHAT TO DO ON YOUR FIRST DATE

- Do something active which forces you to be tactile with each other, such as bowling or ice-skating. Even if you're amazing at bowling, let him win or come to your rescue on the ice and prevent you from falling on your bum. It will really break any shyness between you and you can have a good giggle about it.
- If you are planning to have dinner, go somewhere fun. None of that white-tablecloth stuff! One of those American diners is always crazy and fun – you just have to hope no one comes around with one of those cringey red roses and asks your date to buy you one!
- Avoid anywhere with no atmosphere or where you can hear a pin drop – it will make you both feel really awkward. On the other hand, don't go to a place where you can't hear a thing! You're supposed to be getting to know each other, and how can you do that if you can't hear what he's saying?
- The cinema is always a good option as you can watch something together, get a bit cosy and then discuss it afterwards over a coffee.

WHAT TO WEAR, BEAUTY TIPS AND HOW TO TACKLE YOUR NERVES

- Get plenty of early nights in when you're running up to that first big date. It'll make you look fresh-faced and more alert.

- Avoid eating garlic, onions or anything else that will give you bad breath on the day of your date. No one wants to snog a dustbin! Brush your teeth just before you go out and eat minty chewing gum as a little top-up just before you meet him. Plus chewing gum can actually calm down your nerves.

- While having a relaxing soak in the bath before your date, think about what topics you might want to talk about, in case you get stuck for something to say. Also, have a quick flick through the newspaper or listen to the radio news for any interesting and funny stories.

- Imagine it now… you turning up to a party in your ball gown only to find everyone else is dressed in casual jeans and rocker Ts, cramming in hot dogs and just about to start a game of Twister! You'll feel like a bit of a plonker, right? So, make sure you find out beforehand what the dress code is so you don't turn up looking like a fish out of water. It'll really knock your confidence otherwise.

- Three days before you go out on your date, do a little detox. Eat lots of fruit and vegetables and cut out coffee, tea, all sweets and starchy foods such as bread, which will bloat your stomach. Drink lots of water and herbal tea to flush out toxins, leaving a new and improved you.

- Wear something that makes you feel attractive and comfortable. Over-dressing or showing off too much simply gives the wrong impression. You want your date to take you out and treat you with respect. Remember, the most attractive asset you have is your personality and sense of fun. Set aside some time beforehand to try on lots of outfits to see what makes you look and feel your best.

- Have a little nap before your date. It'll relax you and it's also a good energy boost. Having said that, if you sleep for any longer than 30 minutes, you might feel groggy and not want to go out at all! Oh, and don't forget to set your alarm to wake you up!

- Make sure you leave yourself enough time to get ready so you don't end up rushing and getting your knickers in a twist, leaving you feeling stressed out.

- Put on your favourite CD so that you can sing away while applying your make-up to get you in rock'n'roll mode.

- Presentation is so important, so don't turn up looking like a scruffy Vicky Pollard! Make sure your hair, nails and clothes are all in tip-top condition.

- You may have spent the entire day getting ready, but your date doesn't need to know this! Give him the impression that it all comes naturally and you always look this fab.

- There's nothing more embarrassing than tripping up and falling head over bum! If this happens in front of your date, rather than going red as a radish and making the whole situation even more awkward, laugh and act like you don't care. Be part of the joke, not the joke, if you get my drift. He'll think you're so cool for doing that and he'll laugh with you. Well, hopefully he'll scrape you up off the floor first, with any luck!

- Brush your teeth and always carry a packet of mint chewing gum in your handbag just in case you're in luck with a smooch!

- Sometimes when we get nervous we tighten our shoulders, leaving us looking like a hunchback with no neck. So, to avoid this, think of happy times such as a great holiday or a friend's outrageous birthday party.

- Girlies, it's so much sexier to wear clothes that don't display everything, so wear one hot piece of clothing at a time. Be mysterious and hard to get.

- Wear something that not only suits your personality but

also makes you feel comfortable and super-hot. If you don't, you'll only focus on what feels uncomfortable while pulling and tugging away at whatever it is, rather than concentrating on your date.

- Always wear something that makes you feel confident. You want to be concentrating on your date, not your dress.
- It's always better to under- than overdress. If you feel like a twerp throughout your date, it will affect the way you come across.
- A little bit of text flirting beforehand is a great way of getting to know the person before you go on your first date. You'll both feel less nervous and it will help break the ice.
- Too much make-up is always a no-no! A bit of lippy, a swipe of mascara and some blusher does just the job.

WHEN YOU'RE ON THE DATE...
- For obvious reasons, never order Spaghetti Bolognese. Tomato sauce round your chops is never a good look! If, however, that's the only thing on offer, cut up the pasta strips into little pieces and eat as normal with your fork.
- If you're worried that you might have a little piece of food stuck in your teeth, angle your shiny knife or spoon so you can check on your reflection.
- Worried you might run out of conversation halfway through the evening? If you're a shy girlie, write down some subjects that you love to talk about and stuff the list into your bag. You can always run to the bathroom to swot up!
- Being really late just isn't a 'cool' thing to do. Always aim to be about ten minutes late, no more. Early or on time just makes you look too keen, verging on desperate.
- If the date isn't going too well, don't worry – just look on

it as a learning experience and you'll know what to avoid next time.

- If you find the conversation drying up, then a good thing to do is to ask him a question about himself – boys love to talk about themselves.

- Always be the one to say goodbye first and, if the date went well, take control and get in that driving seat by deciding when the next one will be. Tell him you'll give him a bell.

- If you suffer badly from BO, I strongly recommend you avoid any garlicky or spicy foods – they can cause body odour to increase.

- If you've arrived at the place where you agreed to meet your date but you got caught in a rainstorm, quickly make for the bathroom and stick your head under the hand-dryer. The same goes (within reason!) for wet clothes – take them off and shake under the heat.

- Starting up a fresh conversation with a complete stranger can be really scary at the best of times, so arrange to meet your date in a place where they do really unusual dishes or fabulous and fun drinkies that you can discuss and giggle about.

- Just in case your date goes hideously wrong and you desperately need an excuse to get the hell out, have a friend phone you at a certain time and then pretend to your date that she's in trouble and that you have to go to her rescue!

- You can mention an ex only once. Any more and he'll think that you're still hooked on him!

- Obviously telling a whopper of a lie isn't exactly a good start as all relationships should be based on being honest with each another and lies tend to have a nasty habit of biting us in the bum when we least expect it! Saying that, the odd little white lie here and there to get things going on the conversation front or if you are trying to impress someone is totally harmless. Just remember what you have and haven't said.

- If your date pays you a compliment, take it. If he says you look pretty in what you are wearing, thank him with a cute smile. Confidence and being able to accept a nice comment is such an attractive thing. Maybe you could return the compliment, too?

- Keep the conversation light and fun. Don't delve into his personal life by asking really difficult questions unless he talks about something first.

- If you haven't a clue what to eat, then have a little nosy at what other fellow diners are munching on – it might just give you inspiration.

- If you have lost your appetite because you feel sick with nerves, then suggest how much fun it would be to share a dish. Hopefully, when it turns up, he may just hog the lot and not even notice you haven't really touched it!

- Ordering for each other can be really fun because you then have absolutely no idea what you're going to eat! Just hope he's nice and doesn't order you something disgusting like frogs' legs!

- A little perfume always goes a long way and will be fully appreciated (as long as it doesn't smell like bog cleaner!). The best place to put it is on your pulse points where the blood is very close to the surface (the inner side of your wrists, the temples on the sides of your head and on the side of the front part of your neck) – the skin will be thinner there.

- Guys tend to like confident chicks and the more confident you are, the more you double your chances of dating success. So, if you're lacking in the confidence section, fake it! Eventually it will come naturally.

- Don't be an irritating hyena and chat and laugh so fast and loud that he literally can't hear himself think. Be a cool cat and show off your sense of humour, but with control – it's far more attractive.

- Rather than questions that he can only answer yes or no to, ask him something that he has to give a longer answer to. For example, if you ask him if he likes blue, he may answer yes or no. His favourite childhood memory requires a fuller answer, however.

- If the first date goes well and you want to know whether he's interested or not, mention to him that you have a party in a few weeks' time. If he seems up for it, then he's keen. Assume not if he says he might be busy (mostly he won't be).

- If you think you might be in with a chance of a second date, make sure you find out about his interests and do a bit of research on the computer. When you do meet up again, he'll be well impressed with your fountain of knowledge. This of course is also a great way of making conversation, even if you're not really into what you've just researched!

BEAUTY SOS FOR LAST-MINUTE DATES

So, you're running seriously late because of school or your job, your greasy hair just got rained on because the weather forecast was wrong again and you left your brolly at home. You feel hot and bothered, and it's just typical that this happens on the very day when you've got yourself a date and you've no time to go home first. So, do you cancel? Absolutely not! With just a few sneaky tips you can transform yourself into a babelicious beauty within seconds!

- If your armpits are giving the dustbins a run for their money but you don't have time for a shower, go into the bathroom and wipe them with body wipes or splash some water on them and apply a fresh layer of deodorant. Spritz on some perfume, too. Anything to get rid of that onion whiff!

- If you can't brush your teeth, chew gum or fresh mint, or eat a handful of grapes with a glass of water – this will help spring-clean your mouth.
- When you've got really grubby hair, roughly gather it into a ponytail with your fingertips. A brush will only highlight just how greasy it is. If you have short hair, use a headscarf to hide the grease.
- Oily skin can make you look as if you've had your face stuck in the chip pan all day! Always carry powdered blotting paper (mini sheets of paper coated in fine powder) in your bag to soak up the grease.

KISSING WITH CONFIDENCE

- Make sure your lips are in tip-top condition (see pages 167–69). They need to feel like ice-cream, all soft and scrummy!
- Before you leave the house, make sure you brush your teeth. Now scrape your tongue with the back of a teaspoon to remove any smelly residue that may have got stuck to it. Always pop a packet of mint chewing gum in your handbag just in case a cheeky little smooch does indeed head in your direction later.
- Apply a layer of your fave lipgloss. Don't overdo it, though – you don't want your poor crush to think he's kissing an oil slick, now, do you?
- Smiling, giggling and relaxing are catching, so do all three if you can. This will set the mood for that first perfect pucker.
- Choose a place that's safe, but private. You don't want all your mates barging in and taking the rip out of you.

- A soft, cute kiss on the lips is perfect. If he pushes his tongue down your throat, then hold him back, take control and show him how it's done. Kiss like you want to be kissed. Hopefully, he will follow your lead. And if he doesn't shove his tongue down, then lucky you, he could be a Romeo kisser! Get those lips locked, girl!

- If you want to be totally in the driving seat, then, once you've had your kiss, be the one to walk away. It will drive him crazy – just see!

Handbag essentials for your date

- Minty chewing gum
- Mini bottle of perfume
- Emergency taxi money
- Your mobile
- Lipgloss to make you even more yummy!

SWEET (NOT SICKLY) WAYS TO SHOW HOW YOU FEEL

- Send him a handwritten letter like they used to do in the old days. None of this emailing or texting nonsense! Find some gorgeous writing paper and, using a lovely ink pen, tell him what you think of him and send it to him. He might pretend it's all a bit mushy and try to be all manly, etc., but secretly he'll LOVE it, stash it somewhere safe and get it out every night before he goes to bed to remind himself how lucky he is to have you as his chick!

- Stock up on Love Heart sweets and, when you are next with him, sneak a packet in his jacket pocket or pop some into his bag – a cute little surprise like this will really make his day and I guarantee he won't be able to think of anything else but you.

- Hold a fixed gaze with a small, yet warm smile when you're talking to him. Now, I don't mean one of the looks you use when you're playing that staring game, just something that's romantic and loving.

- Take some pics on your mobile from a really memorable place (this could be the park by the pond, for example) and then use this as wallpaper for your mobile. Every time you're together, you can show him and have a good old giggle about it.

- Organise a little picnic, so it's just the two of you. Make sure you choose all of his favourite things so that he knows you've really put some thought into it.

- Compliment him from time to time. It could be at how good he is at footie or tell him you love what he's wearing. Trust me, boys love to be the centre of attention – it massages their egos and makes them feel good. Having said that, don't do this too often or his head might grow too big so he won't be able to fit through the door!

- Make him feel special. Give him a little surprise hug when he's least expecting it and, when he asks why you did that, just say because you felt like it and because he's a special guy. Just remember, your body language says a million things. The warmer and friendlier you are, the more he'll be with you.

- Saying 'I love you' can be really hard, right? For some reason, saying it in French is a lot easier to do without being cringey. Don't ask me why! Anyway, this is how you say it: 'Je t'aime'.

MEETING THE PARENTS

It's all about first impressions, girlies. Believe you me, they count and they're long-lasting, too! Arrive dressed as an elegant young lady complete with charming manners and delightful chat and you might just find yourself being invited on the family holiday. Follow my tips and go down a treat with his nearest and dearest.

- A bit of cheesy sucking-up never does any harm, so take over a box of choccies or a little bunch of flowers.
- Dress like a young lady, not some flesh-baring punk rocker about to go out clubbing – this will only leave his parents wide-eyed with shock and wondering who on earth he's brought home. Leave the micro mini in your wardrobe!
- Opt for something more on the smart, but casual side of things – for instance, a pair of dark jeans with a cute little top, or even a pretty little dress. Remember, first impressions count big time.
- You might have a thing for tattoos and piercings, but not everyone else does! So, keep these little artistic delights out of sight until you get to know his family better.
- Your make-up should be fresh-faced and fanciful. Not vampish and caked on like an acrylic painting – I'm sure they'd like to see your true features!
- The second that you come face to face with his parents stand tall and introduce yourself confidently. Stick your hand out for a good old friendly handshake.
- Don't try to impress too much. Be yourself and relax. They'll love you for who you are. If you try to put on a front, they'll see straight through it.
- Don't smother him in affection right in front of them. Yep, that means no sticking your tongue down his throat and trying to snog his face off while you're in the same room as them. They'll simply see this as disrespectful. Instead, just give him a secret smile.

269

- Be polite and don't forget to say please and thank you.
- Ask his parents a few questions to find out more about what they're into and what their hobbies are.
- And finally, just pretend you're interested in what they say, no matter how much they may drone on. Just grit your teeth and remember it's not for long.

INVITING YOUR NEW BOYFRIEND OVER TO MEET YOUR PARENTS

These cringeworthy situations can swing either way. Your hot new crush will either leave after dinner loving you even more because your parents and younger siblings have acted totally cool and made you look even cooler, or he'll be falling over himself to get out of the house as quickly as possible because he's spent the last two hours being force-fed stories about you and because your mum thought it would be a good idea to show him all of your baby photos. So you not only spend most of your evening wishing you could hide under a rock, but also looking like a giant red radish because you're nervously sweating like an out-of-control garden sprinkler!

- Firstly, if you have a little brother you need to have a word with him. Telling embarrassing stories to put your date off you will more than likely be his priority. So either pay him off with some of your savings or take away his favourite toy and tell him he will only get it back if he behaves.
- Hide all family albums, so that your mum won't be tempted to whip them out after dinner.
- Before he comes over, ask him what he does and doesn't like to eat. He may be allergic to or really hate the taste of something. You want him to enjoy this cringey experience as much as possible.

HOW TO GET OUT OF THE NEXT DATE

He's super-keen on you and you just want to run a mile leaving a big bucket of vomit behind you... Well, there's one way you can get rid of him, and that is to behave like a minger.

- Pick your nose or teeth in front of him.
- Blow the bogies out of your nose using the napkin on the table.
- Swap your normal laugh for a really annoying horse 'neighying' one.
- Keep your armpits and legs lovely and hairy.
- When putting on your lipstick, smudge it all around the edges.
- Eat garlic the night before so your breath stinks! Oh yes, and don't brush your teeth before you meet him.
- Forget to put any BO basher on. Make sure you go for a sweaty run beforehand so that you really stink of onions.

If all else fails, you could simply treat him as you yourself would like to be treated. Either arrange to meet him and tell him that you would rather just be friends or pick up the phone and explain the situation then. NEVER do it via text – it's lame and weak and that's how he will remember you (think how you would feel if he dumped you by text – cheesed off, right?).

HEAL YOUR BROKEN HEART

There aren't many things that hurt more than having your heart smashed into a million pieces by the cute guy that you've totally fallen for. One moment he's unbelievably adorable and caring, the next he's dumping you by text, totally out of the blue. So, what's all that about? It's at this point that your whole life feels like it's tumbling down and the thought of having to pick up the pieces and put them back together just seems impossible and out of the question when all you can think about is his sweet blue eyes and his cute way of answering the phone to you. But stop right there! Don't torture yourself because this is the start of an exciting new chapter, much better than the last. So, go down to your local supermarket and buy lots of tissues. Now go home, lock yourself in the bedroom and cry him out of your system. The quicker you get it all out, the faster you will heal. Here's how to bounce back in style.

- First things, first: speed dial was invented to phone our nearest and dearest in times of need. Whenever I've split, I've put that speed-dial button into full-throttle action so my best friend Emily's there in minutes on the doorstep, clutching a tub of Ben & Jerry's, a good selection of chick flicks, a box of tissues and, most importantly, a huge hug.
- Instead of sitting around sulking because that good-for-nothing has dumped you, do something positive instead. Not only will this distract you and help take your mind off him, but it will help put a positive spin on the whole thing, therefore making the healing process a lot easier and quicker.
- Never leave the house without looking hotter than hot. Bumping into him with red crying eyes and daggy clothes won't make him feel gutted that you two have split. Turn up the style factor and look drop-dead gorge, even if you're just popping over the road to get a pint of milk! Oh, and don't forget the big WAG glasses – they're brill for hiding red puffy eyes.
- One of the best ways of getting over a guy is to think of all his bad points, not the good ones. It's so easy to zone in on

his cute little smile and his infectious laugh, but this will only make you feel worse. Instead, remind yourself of what an idiot he was, and how he really didn't want to mix with your friends and how you hated his favourite trainers. This kind of constructive thinking will get you over him in no time at all.

- Give yourself a mini makeover. A bit of girly pampering will instantly make you feel a whole lot better about yourself. Try some new make-up looks, get your mum or best friend to blow-dry your hair into a hot Hollywood style, and of course, what's a pampering session without a mani and pedi? See pages 188–97.

- Keep yourself busy and occupied. Take up a new hobby, see a funny film, bake cakes with your family or organise a clothes-swapping session with the chicks (see pages 17-20). Anything just to keep your mind off him and on something else! Eventually, you'll be so busy you won't think of him anyway.

- Try not to stay in contact with him for now – it's the best way to preserve a friendship, if that's what you want. The odd little text here or there will just keep the wound open and cause further pain. Cut him off totally so you can start a fresh new life without him.

- During this emotional time, have your nearest and dearest around you for support and comfort – they too will want you to heal quickly and will listen to you till they're blue in the face! That's what friends are for – and besides when they go through the same thing you can help them through a sticky time too.

- Delete all messages from him – re-reading loving texts will only cause further heartbreak.

- Get rid of all of his emails. In fact, do your best to forget his address altogether! The more you rid yourself of his details, the less tempted you will be to contact him when you're having a low moment.

- Put any little pressies that he gave you and even any photos in a box and hide them up in the attic until you feel ready and comfortable to be around them again – I swear this really will speed up the healing process.

- It's good to have a little cry every day as it helps relieve the stress. If you don't let all your hurt out and you just bottle it up, then it may just come back and haunt you. All I can say is, the hurt won't go on forever. One day you'll just stop and you'll feel this amazing sense of freedom and start seeing the joy in life again.

- Exercise is one of the best healing medicines ever! Not only does it help lift your mood, but you'll also feel fitter and more attractive. Watch out, boys!

- Remember, laughter is the best medicine, so arm yourself with your bez mate, your fave tub of ice cream and, of course, a funny film.

MEETING YOUR EX'S NEW GIRL

You so want her not to be cooler, taller or prettier than you, don't you? Ideally, she'll be no threat at all, with big black curly teeth, rank chat, brainless, with sad friends and clothes so minging you could almost mistake her for a tent on legs! OK, so your ex obviously has good taste, otherwise why would he have gone out with you? Which is why there's always a risk that it might not be long before he has another hot chick on his arm. So, what do you do when you come face to face with his new sweetheart? Do you accidentally spill your drink over her irritatingly super-cool outfit, or quickly grab a hot boy from the dancefloor, superglue him to your arm (even if you don't know him, any fittie will do), hold your head high and stick an 'I'm over him and moved on' smile? Much as you might love to chuck a drink over her, or stick a chip to her bum so that everyone can laugh at her, it's so much cooler to act like you really don't care and put on a happy face. Here's how to handle this tricky situation.

- Firstly, never look like you've tried to out-dress her. Let her think you're a naturally cool cat with effortless style (even though you've spent the last two weeks preparing and planning what to wear!).
- Avoid making any catty remarks about your ex to her face. You'll only come across as a sad and jealous type.
- Make her have hair envy! The night before, sleep with olive oil in your hair so it gleams like silk and get the best blow-dry ever!
- Always wear high heels – you'll look far more powerful and in control.
- Each time she looks over at you, make sure you're having a blast even if you feel gutted inside that he's with her, not you. Let her think you're the one that everyone wants to be around.

So, all you Lazy Princesses: you've read it, you've tried it, you've tested it. Use this book to lead you to utter perfection and remember: if there's a shortcut to a glam goal, then take it! Good luck, lovely ladies!

Lazy Princess Shopping List

Fashion

CLOTHES

- Tk maxx – it's officially paradise – if you haven't experienced it, then you haven't lived. If you can't find me, I'm usually hanging out here!
- Primark – cheap and cheerful and brilliant
- Oasis – it's heaven on toast
- Lipsy – it's a one-stop shop where you are guaranteed to pick up handfuls of to-die-for goodies (found in Topshop)
- Gap – the place to stock up on staples such as jeans and Ts
- French Connection – the place to get your winter coats
- H&M – brilliant for the basics and funky nick-nacks
- Vanilla (Kings Road, London) – while you're in there browsing for your winter gilet, don't be surprised if you bump into a celeb, they love this place
- Zara – get involved, is all I can say. It's the cheap version of Prada
- Topshop – it's basically an Aladdin's cave for fashion addicts. Best babe bikinis too!

- Miss Selfridge – bang-on-trend wardrobe fillers from street to bo-ho chic
- All Saints – this place has Kate Moss written all over it!
- Warehouse – always has a little party frock problem-fixer in store
- Urban Outfitters – the place for retro-looking Ts
- River Island – if you like to stalk style, then cruise on down to here

UNDERWEAR

- By Caprice lingerie (www.bycapricelingerie.com) – if you see it, get it! Everything is uber girly and uber cool! They're an absolute must-have
- Topshop – reams and reams of every style in every colour. If you can't find anything here, then your underwear drawer is doomed
- Pussy Glamour – found in Topshop, Figleaves (www.figleaves.com) and Selfridges – trust me, this is the hottest brand out there. With faces such as Alice Dellal and Rosie Huntington-Whiteley appearing in the ads, this is a sure way of adding 'the real deal' of rock and roll to your wardrobe
- M&S – OK, so your granny might do her underwear shopping here too, but don't let that put you off. M&S is bursting at the seams with gorgeous girly undies for all shapes and sizes!
- Tesco – treat yourself to a little selection of fun new undies
- Jonathon Aston tights at mytights.com – oodles of jewel-coloured tights for every occasion

Lazy Princess Shopping List

ACCESSORIES

- The Earring Boutique – yummy yummy ear decorations!
- Freedom at Topshop – it's the equivalent of being trapped in a sweet shop! You want everything!
- Accessorize – I could easily spend a whole day in here!
- Urban Outfitters – hip retro gear for the edgy crew!
- Claire's Accessories – everything from fairy wings to bling bangles
- Aldo – great funky bits here
- penshop.co.uk – you could try here for a funky passport cover online
- H.Samuel – if a special birthday is coming up, then try to steer your parents in this direction. Great watches and bracelets

SHOES

- Wedgewelly.co.uk – check out this website for your Glastonbury staple – your wellies! The perfect footwear for the fashionistas out there!
- Office – bundles of goodies from glam boots to sporty trainers
- Topshop – shoe heaven!
- Ugg Australia – it's as if your feet never left your cosy bed! They're the ultimate in squidgyness and an A-list celeb must-have. If they're good enough for Sienna Miller and Lily Allen, then they're good enough for us too!
- Moda in Pelle – if you want a bit of catwalk couture that won't break the bank, then this is where you need to be shopping!

FACE

- Simple cleansing wipes from Boots – remove all old make-up in one neat whoosh!
- amie New Leaf Skin Exfoliating Polish – cleanses and revives dull looking skin (perfect for after a party)
- amie Petal Perfect Refreshing Cleansing Lotion – AMAZING for fresh skin! Girlies, stock up on this stuff! Trust me!
- amie Spring Clean Cooling Clay Mask – heavenly after a hard week's studying at school. The peppermint and lime butter just makes your skin buzz with energy.
- Grace Your Face Tea Tree Blemish cover stick – covers up grim-looking spots while feeding them goodness at the same time
- Bliss Fabulous Foaming Face Wash – I use this day and night, and I definitely credit it with giving me crystal-clear skin
- Good Skin Clean Skin Foaming Cleanser – works wonders for cleaning a city grubbed-up face

BODY

- Vichy Auto Bronzant – for a golden glow, this is the fake tan to go for
- M&S exfoliating gloves – they are brilliant for removing dead skin cells if you are going to be chucking on a layer of fake tan
- Rimmel Sun Shimmer – instant tan cream for your face and body. I use it on my leggies if they are looking a bit pasty white and I have to wear a short skirt or dress. When you get back home later, don't forget to wash it off in the shower, otherwise you will wake up and your white bed sheets will have turned the brown!

- Soap and Glory Sugar Crush Body Scrub – it's a flaky skin fighter. This scrumptious smashed brown sugar and sweet lime oil scrub is nothing less than pure delight to smear all over your body. (As an alternative, though, you can always use a mixture of brown sugar and olive oil.)

HANDS

- Adcal D3 – these calcium tablets make your nails rock solid and long. You can get them in most pharmacies
- Lemon and Zest Hand Wipes from M&S – handy to have in your handbag for when you need to clean your mitts
- OPI nail lacquers – they really 'hit the nail on the head' every time. The colours are fab and, what's more, they just don't chip
- One-coat fast-finish nail polish by No 17
- Neal's Yard Pumice Foot Scrub – for sparkling tootsies
- Bliss softening socks – if your feet are rougher than sandpaper, then you need to get them back to their former glory. You simply pop these little socks on for 20 minutes and the gel inside cuddles and soothes them, taking away all of the dryness.
- Bliss Glamour Gloves – these gel-lined beauty gloves soften and glamorise rough hands
- Gosh nail lacquer – give your nails a makeover with hot acid shades

HANDS AND FEET

- Gillette Venus Breeze – it's the Rolls-Royce of the razor world. All Gillette razors are, but the Venus Breeze is particularly brilliant because it comes with a built-in gel bar, meaning you don't have to lug foam around with you, plus it gives your shave a smoother feel

HAIR

- Batiste – dry shampoo for when you can't be bothered to wash your hair!
- L'Oreal Volume Extra – an excellent hair mousse that keeps your hair looking salon sexy and polished
- Soap and Glory Hair Supply – a super-gloss treat for your locks
- Richard Ward Ultimate Repair Mask from Superdrug. It gives you instant Hannah Montana glam locks. I wash mine, then sleep in the stuff and wash it out the next day! How easy is that!
- Tangle Teezer – available from Boots. If your hair resembles overcooked spaghetti, then get one of these. They'll tease and squeeze all of those unwanted tangles right out of sight!

TEETH

- Oral B Triumph electric toothbrush – cleans your pegs like a Dyson vacuum cleans the floor!
- Oral B dental floss – sets free those trapped snacks
- Colgate Advanced Whitening toothpaste – leaves your teeth sparking like diamonds

Make-up-bag essentials

- Max Factor mascaras – no make-up bag is complete without one of these wedged in there somewhere
- Bourjois Line Effect – liquid heaven for your lashes
- Nivea Caregloss and Shine (natural colour) – fantastic for a princess pout
- Liparazzi – officially the most fun lipgloss in the universe. Comes complete with a built-in mirror, light and lippy! How cool is that?

- Fake eyelashes from Boots – Beyonce, eat your heart out!
- Tweezerman – the best tweezers for zapping away those stray hairs
- Tampax compak – always best to be prepared
- Fairy Dust eau de parfum by Paris Hilton. Available from Macy's

Cures

- 4 head – great for annoying headaches

Gadgets

- Sony digital picture frame – exclusive to M&S. You can load all of your photos on to it and watch them flick through!
- ghd hair straighteners from ghdhair.com – for feline flicks then invest in a set of these
- www.red5.co.uk– this really is the ultimate gadget shop. Brilliant for birthday pressies for your buddies!
- Roberts Rd-50 Revival DAB digital radio. It comes in pink and is soooo funky!

Pressies for your Crush

- Paperchase – squillions of cards from lovey dovey to hysterically funny
- Love Hearts – available in all sweet shops
- Digital photo keychain from Convenient Gadgets – remind him how fab you are with this digi picture frame which dangles on a key chain. You can put your best pics on there for him to flip through when he's not with you! You can load 60 images on to this little baby!

Princess Must-haves

- *Mizz* magazine – this is your bible for everything, girlies. If you haven't read it, then boy have you missed out big time!
- Nesquik chocolate-flavoured milkshake/hot chocolate powder! This is the best stress-buster of all time, and the perfect little treat for after school

A WORD ABOUT OUR COMPETITION WINNERS

The drawings that appear alongside each chapter in *The Lazy Princess* are the winning entries from a competition that was held in schools across the country for 11–16-year-olds. Participating pupils were asked to draw a picture to illustrate a particular chapter of *The Lazy Princess*.

We would like to thank the schools for taking part in the competition. Congratulations to the winners, who will receive a signed copy of *The Lazy Princess*. Each winner's school will also be visited by the Lazy Goddess herself, Hannah Sandling, who will give a talk on the quick and easy way to look amazing and be fabulous at everything.